# BFI Modern Classics

**Rob White**
Series Editor

BFI Modern Classics is a series of critical studies of films produced over the last three decades. An array of writers explore their chosen films, offering a range of perspectives on the dominant art and entertainment medium in contemporary culture. The series gathers together snapshots of our passion for and understanding of recent movies.

### Also Published

**L.A. Confidential**
Manohla Dargis

(see a full list of titles in the series at the back of this book)

### Forthcoming

**Amores Perros**
Paul Julian Smith

**The Shawshank Redemption**
Mark Kermode

# The Idiots

**John Rockwell**

 Publishing

First published in 2003 by the
**British Film Institute**
21 Stephen Street, London W1T 1LN

Copyright © John Rockwell 2003

The British Film Institute promotes greater
understanding and appreciation of,
and access to, film and moving image
culture in the UK.

British Library Cataloguing-in-Publication Data
A catalogue record for this book is available
from the British Library

ISBN 0-85170-955-9

Series design by Andrew Barron &
Collis Clements Associates

Typeset in Italian Garamond and Swiss 721BT
by D R Bungay Associates, Burghfield, Berks

Printed in Great Britain by
Cromwell Press, Trowbridge, Wiltshire

# Contents

## Prologue: The Shock

There are times watching a movie that you can't believe what you are seeing on the screen: you can't believe that an actor would push a performance so far, that a director would take such a risk. This can't go on, you fear, dreading and hoping it will, if you have time to think about it at all. Something will snap; the tension will collapse like a stage set to reveal the bare backstage walls behind the art.

I felt that way the first time I saw the final scene of Lars von Trier's *The Idiots*. A drab, bourgeois house is filled with the intensity of silence. The quiet centre of the film, Karen, the woman with a terrible secret who has spent two weeks as the bemused and gradually seduced outsider in a commune of young upper-class Danes out to shock society by pretending to be idiots, to 'spass', has gone home. She wants to prove the therapeutic, not to say moral, rightness of the crackpot theories of the increasingly deranged group leader, Stoffer – that something good will come of 'spassing' in front of those closest to you.

What follows proceeds with the inexorability of a Greek tragedy, except that Karen's final act of transgression seems in retrospect like a triumph. You watch the screen like you'd watch a snake, fearful that it will strike at you. How far will, or can, Karen – or the actress playing her, Bodil Jørgensen, or von Trier himself, the writer and director and cameraman behind this unbearable intensity – push things?

It's as if the whole impassioned, comical, serious, provocative, influential essence of the Dogma 95 manifesto had been invented for this scene. It sweeps up the viewer (it swept me up), it rewards continuous reviewings, it validates an aesthetic, it makes one fearful how any actor could be so emotionally exposed and how any director could surgically peel back her and our normal human defences to reveal such agonised depths. And it gives a powerful sense of how von Trier's enormous talents and sometimes scary methodology might be turned to projects that stretch far beyond Dogma intimacy.

Von Trier was the instigator of the Dogma 'brotherhood' and has said that no director should make more than one strictly Dogma film. With a couple of minor skirtings of Dogma strictures, *The Idiots* is his one Dogma film. It is the least known among his mature films: this is a movie in Danish, cast at least in part with unknowns even in that country and with ample nudity, erections and a 'penetration shot'. Not just because of the sex but because of the roughness and tastelessness, it is also his most controversial film, which is saying something in a career filled with controversy, his weirdest and – it seems still despite the enthusiasm that any project arouses at the moment of creation – his favourite.

It is also about the most documented film in cinematic history, at least if you know Danish and Swedish (which I don't) and French (which I do). Thankfully von Trier hasn't followed through on his promise/threat to release every take (130 hours worth in this case) on the internet, so that anyone with a computer could make their own cut; copyright reasons are the problem, he says.

Aside from a fair number of interviews and press conferences and several books with sections on the film, *The Idiots* has also been memorialised in Jesper Jergil's documentary from the innermost inside, *The Humiliated* (1998), which follows the making of the film with subtitled voiceovers by von Trier reading from a journal he recorded nearly every night during the six-week shoot and subsequent post-production. And in a book, first in Danish and then translated into French, containing an edited but still far more complete version of the *Idiots* journal, 72 densely printed pages in the French version, plus von Trier's original screenplay, which despite

Von Trier directing the pool scenes

considerable improvisation during the shoot wound up pretty close to the finished film. True to the quick and simple Dogma spirit, he proudly claims he wrote it in four days. But he later conceded that the writing had been the result of a couple of years of cogitation.

But what do we really know about von Trier and this film after digesting all this verbiage? At one point in his journal, he wearily complains of 'a day filled with words, words and words, and eventually demolished by words'. It can be said that *The Idiots*, von Trier's ugly duckling that posterity seems to be recognising as a swan, is a movie about movies, a movie about acting, a movie about life, a movie about provocation and morality, a movie about sexuality and compassion, a movie about the Dogma 'brotherhood', and a step along the way to something entirely different in von Trier's overflowing artistic imagination: the use of Dogma chastity to explore the sensual excesses of first the musical (*Dancer in the Dark*) and now Wagner's four-opera *Ring* cycle, which he will direct at the Wagner shrine at Bayreuth in Bavaria starting in 2006.

Although before that there is *Dogville*, his first movie with Hollywood stars, and then two sequels to that film, the first called *Mandalay*. Up to now, von Trier has worked in trilogies, but at first, before the idea of a Kidman–*Dogville* trilogy sprang into his brain, he allowed that *Dogville* could be considered part of the same grouping as *Breaking the Waves* (1996), *The Idiots* (1998) and *Dancer in the Dark* (2000). Which would have made a tetralogy, but that would have been OK: von Trier likes tetralogies, too, given his forthcoming assault on Wagner's *Ring*. But now, with Kidman aboard, it's back to trilogies.

Whatever, von Trier is typically full of energy and ambition, painting his canvases on bigger and bigger screens. He is no longer just Denmark's; he is the world's. And one could argue that this leap into world prominence, in film and beyond, had its roots not just in his student days and earlier work, but in Dogma and his little Danish Dogma film, *The Idiots*. Dogma was a manifesto that levelled the ground in preparation for the construction of new and grander edifices. *The Idiots* is a film with a quirky subject and a troubled process of creation that reaches down into unforeseen depths of emotion and catharsis, yet points the way forward beyond itself.

## 1 *The Idiots*

After the Dogma certificate and a crudely drawn title, *The Idiots* begins
with a sad-looking woman, pretty but plain – her name, we soon discover,
is Karen – at a carnival sideshow. The barker, spinning a wheel in some
kind of game of chance, says, 'The tension mounts, hits the roof and falls
to earth with a bang' (all dialogue citations from the English subtitles).

Then suddenly she is riding, still alone, in a horse-drawn carriage
through a Copenhagen park, her face a dazed blank, the gentle clip-
clopping far from the racket of the sideshow, accompanied by a sad tune
on a melodica. (Mostly there is no background music except for found
sound; this tune, which recurs sparingly, is all there is.) Then, abruptly,
she's asking about the prawns at a proper middle-class restaurant.

Already, in these first 32 seconds, we know that this will be an
austere, determinedly rough movie. Von Trier was his own cameraman,
90 per cent of the time, shooting hand-held video. From an American
perspective, a lot of low-budget European movies look technically raw,
and Dogma just pushes that extreme further. They concentrate on close-
ups and conversation rather than polished craft, let alone slick spectacle.
Von Trier's own earlier films had often self-consciously experimented with
colour and atmosphere (see *The Element of Crime*, with its persistent
beige). No such danger here – no danger of one's attention being
distracted by filmic virtuosity from character and dialogue, ideas and
emotion.

At the restaurant, it turns out Karen hasn't enough money for more
than a simple salad. The waiter, outwardly solicitous, asks if she can afford
mineral water, or would prefer water 'from the tap'. She chooses the
mineral water. The cut to her sitting bemusedly at her table, toying with
her water, is again almost brutal in its abruptness, the sound from the
previous shot chopped off.

Her attention is drawn to a nearby table, at which sits an angularly
handsome blond man (Stoffer, short for Kristoffer) drinking orange juice
and a pretty young woman (Susanne); all seems normal. Karen's salad
arrives. Then things begin to go off the rails, in terms of the hushed

politesse expected at a restaurant like this at Sunday brunch. Susanne tries to spoon-feed Stoffer a bite of something; he twists his head back, crying 'No' with a mixture of anger and fear. A bearded man at their table (Henrik) is fumbling to figure out how to eat his food, with little success. Karen watches all this.

Stoffer pushes Susanne away, knocking crockery off the table, which breaks. He stands up, Susanne trying to make him pick up his mess. Stoffer wanders about the restaurant, using people's napkins and saying 'Hi' to everyone, to their evident consternation. The bearded man starts crying, and Susanne comforts him. When Stoffer reaches Karen's table and says 'Hi' to her, she responds with a 'Hi' of her own, hushed with tenderness, her face a timid but radiant smile.

The waiter is becoming concerned, 'for the other diners'. Henrik wanders out and is led back by Susanne. Stoffer grows louder and Susanne capitulates, trying to get him to go without too big a scene. He shouts 'No'. Suddenly he is clutching Karen's hand. She agrees to go outside with him, presumably to facilitate his acquiescence.

Outside, the 'Klaus' whom Susanne has mentioned is about to come and get them turns out to be a plain old taxi. The two men get in the back, Stoffer still holding Karen's hand. Susanne loses her temper, but then we're in the taxi and it's moving and Karen is sitting next to Stoffer, still holding hands with him. The hand-held camera, shot from the front passenger seat, is as jerky as the ride; the lighting is natural to the point of obfuscation, the two men's faces deep in shadow.

We cut to a reverse shot from the rear of Susanne in the front; she's angry and tired of the antics in the restaurant. The two men look at each other with idiot blankness and then burst out laughing. Karen shrinks in her seat, no longer holding Stoffer's hand. Stoffer apologises to Susanne but says what else were they to do? The dinner would have cost them a fortune. The taxi driver, assured that they do have the money for the fare, drives on towards the suburbs. Susanne slaps Stoffer's knee affectionately, and they all laugh. So what we (and Karen) know so far is that the two men aren't really retarded and that Susanne is in on their game.

There is a sudden cut (all cuts in the *The Idiots* are sudden) to the first of nine short documentary-style interludes, wherein members of what we soon discover was a kind of commune, disbanded before the documentary footage was shot, look back on their experiences, sometimes prodded by an off-camera voice (von Trier's). No one is interviewed with another former member of the group. Neither Karen, the late-arriving outsider, nor Stoffer, the commune leader and her antipode in the film's structure, appear in the documentaries.

In this first one, commune members – Jeppe, a baby-faced innocent; Henrik; and Josephine, a sweet ingénue – say Karen was the last to join their group and that she was always a bit of an outsider and Ped (a psychiatrist normally seen sucking his pipe and taking notes about the group's 'experiment') says that Karen was right in constantly questioning them about their 'poking fun' at the outside world.

The taxi arrives at the group's suburban home in the fashionable upper-middle-class suburb of Søllerød (a five-minute walk from von Trier's own home). Others are already preparing for a planned outing to visit a factory: Ped getting into the wheelchair he doesn't need, etc., the wheelchair pushed by Miguel, an immigrant. Stoffer greets the others, idiotically.

Quick cut to the Rockwool insulation factory, where an earnest, polite, blue-overalled guide meets them. Karen stands apart in the far distance, but is fetched by Miguel. Cut to the group milling about among dangerous-looking machines dressed in orange jackets and hard hats. They push buttons, react with terror or pleasure at various demonstrations, deliberately decide *en masse* that a shivering cartoon house is the one properly insulated, and so forth. 'That was almost right,' says the kindly tour guide, although he does seem rather eager in the end for them to leave ('I think I hear your mini-bus,' extricating himself from Stoffer's bear-hug). He looks non-plussed when he realises that Ped is in the driver's seat ('Responsibility does them good,' Susanne explains sweetly). The mini-bus ricochets around the parking lot, bouncing off neatly stacked piles of Rockwool, and finally putters down the driveway.

Cut to the interior of the van, where everyone is singing that their chauffeur is a 'nutter'. Stoffer asks Karen what she thinks of it all. She says

Clockwise from top left: Jeppe, Ped, Josephine, Katrine, Nana, Miguel, Axel, Henrik

she doesn't think what they did was very funny; that they poke fun. After a pause, Stoffer says bitterly that 'they' are the ones who poke fun; the others calm him down.

Of course, they *are* poking fun; that's the point, or if not the point, then the tactic they use to contrast themselves with what they see as a self-satisfied and hypocritical bourgeoisie. But when Karen says she doesn't think it was very funny, she is not just echoing the reaction of many who see this film and find the so-called idiots' antics distasteful. The idiots all seem to be well enough off to spend all their time at the commune, although periodic intimations of the outside world intrude: Stoffer is supposedly trying to sell the house on behalf of his uncle; Axel is on paternity leave from his advertising agency, though he spends precious little time at home with his wife and baby; Ped is a doctor undertaking a research project; Henrik is an art teacher on leave; money, to judge from their inability to pay their restaurant bill, can run short.

But Karen is also doing more than question their motives. She is establishing the two contrasting elements of this film, the two arcs whose intersection gives it drama. The stunts with the bourgeoisie continue, but gradually the tragic, emotional side of the film emerges, steadily and inexorably, until Karen incarnates its shattering climax.

In that sense the provocations of the idiots can be seen (enjoyed?) as dark comedy – and some of the scenes, as with the van careening around the Rockwool parking lot – are indeed funny. Or they can be seen as a protracted, delayed setup for the ending, with the scenes of emotion and vulnerability, of terror, tragedy and triumph, gradually supplanting the cavortings, allowing them to form the 'light' foil for their darkness – or maybe it's just different shades of dark.

The group arrives home, boisterous and business-as-usual. Axel lends Karen a mobile phone. She withdraws to a side room, closing the door, and places a call to 'Anders', birds chirping from the garden. Presumably she has had thoughts of returning to wherever it is she came from. But when he asks, 'Is that you, Karen?' she hangs up, weeping and moaning to herself, like a wounded doe.

A night-time discussion, by candlelight (which means everyone is pretty much lost in the gloom unless directly illuminated by a candle; von Trier struggles to keep the images in focus, but they fuzz in and out). The group, led by Stoffer, analyses its performances as idiots at Rockwool. Stoffer tears into Jeppe as being hopelessly unconvincing. Others, led by Axel, defend him. Susanne suggests that Karen spend the night, but Karen says she won't sleep there; she just wants 'to sit a while'.

Second documentary interlude: Axel is flummoxed when the off-camera von Trier asks him for a 'quick summary' of what the group was up to. Axel's wife, sitting near him, says he just wanted to get laid, as often and as variously as possible. There is confusion as to whose idea the group was originally – Axel's? Stoffer's? Jeppe's? – though everyone admits that Stoffer became the leader. Susanne thinks Stoffer would not admit it was all a game, but that it really was.

The next morning, Karen wakes up having slept next to Susanne on the floor. Everyone is having breakfast in the garden, some of them 'spassing' – their term for acting the idiot and just as rude in Danish as it is in English. Katrine, with whom Axel has been having an affair, arrives, having gone to Jutland for a break. She tells Axel she went because she thought their spassing was 'pathetic', but that she's come back because she's changed her mind. Axel accuses her of being hung up on him. Stoffer accepts her version, and she's welcomed back.

Everyone is packing up for an outing. Jeppe is struggling to tie Ped's collapsible wheelchair to the top of a car, ineptly even though he isn't in idiot mode; much discussion about knots. Susanne worries that things shouldn't get rough because the pool can be slippery, and protests that she always has to be the 'minder'; Karen, hovering in the doorway, agrees to help in the minding. As they walk toward the pool, more fretting from Karen about 'poking fun'.

At the pool, they all act like children. Ped swims with about five floats buoying him up. Nana, the hard-boiled sexpot of the group, who never really tries to spass, pretends to have trouble putting on her swimsuit top, which keeps falling off. She then chastises the men and boys who have been having fun helping her, calling on her 'husband', Ped, to defend her honour, which he does, acting idiotically. Axel tries to talk with Katrine about their relationship while they throw a ball back and forth; Katrine keeps acting the idiot.

In the women's shower – where Stoffer goes because he won't let go of Karen's hand – Stoffer, surrounded by naked women and being washed by Karen and then Susanne, gets an erection.

Third documentary: A discussion of why Karen stayed, given her evident discomfiture. Ped says 'she needed us badly.'

A verdant forest idyll, all green and birds chirping and a heavenly shot upwards into the canopy. The idiots are collecting twigs and branches (which they will eventually fashion into ugly Christmas ornaments). There is a long – for this film, where everything is clipped and compact – discussion between Karen and Stoffer as to the meaning of the group, which turns out to be a pretty half-baked, satiric assemblage of post-1960s' protest ideas.

Karen: 'Why do you do it?' Stoffer, pontificating as he puffs on a cigar: 'They're searching for their inner idiot, Karen … What's the idea of a society that gets richer and richer – when it doesn't make anyone happier? In the stone age, right, all the idiots died. It doesn't have to be like that nowadays. Being an idiot is a luxury, but it is also a step forward. Idiots are the people of the future. If one can find the one idiot that happens to be one's own idiot … ' Karen: 'But there are people who are really ill. It's sad for the people who are not able like us. How can you … how can you justify acting the idiot?' Stoffer: 'You can't.'

Karen: ' I would just like to understand. I mean … ' Stoffer, his arm around Karen's shoulder: 'Understand what?' Karen: 'Why I'm here. Why I am here.' Stoffer, pointing flirtatiously at her belly: 'Perhaps it's because there's a little idiot in there that wants to come out and have company' – which in retrospect is a harrowing, inadvertently cruel foreshadowing of the film's great secret.

Jeppe nuzzles Josephine. There is a comic scene in which Nana, sunbathing topless, borrows mayonnaise from a table of picnicking strangers to use as tanning lotion for her breasts. Jeppe slides awkwardly down a snow-less ski jump and is first carried off in triumph, then covered with greenery and affection by the group, to the accompaniment of the melodica tune. A dog barks in the distance; Karen looks tentatively happy.

Fourth documentary: The group has splintered; no one is in contact with anyone else, and some of them regret it. Josephine, looking blank – heartbreaking in light of their subsequent love scene – says she hasn't spoken with Jeppe ('He was all right … ') or anyone else. Katrine says they were a family, 'damn it'. Nana portrays herself as 'on the outside, but not emotionally. Because I loved them all, and they know it.' Henrik wonders sadly, 'Maybe we just weren't so strong together as we thought.'

Stoffer is awakened by Miguel with the news that Axel is outside throwing rocks through the shed's windows. Stoffer's uncle Svend arrives, curious to see how much progress his nephew has made selling his house; Stoffer explains for the first time to the group that the house is not really his but that he's borrowed it until he sells it. The idiots, all acting idiotically, are characterised by Stoffer as trained craftsmen, brought in to fix up the place, which looks spotless, except for them. Everyone's a craftsman – even Jeppe, the 'gardener', who is vacuuming the stones in the patio, and the voluptuous Nana, wandering about naked, and Ped, who is pulling down the 'For Sale' sign, and Axel, still throwing rocks through shed windows. The uncle warns Stoffer to take his job of selling the place seriously.

A short scene, only 51 seconds, but the first of the almost terrifying emotional depths that shift the entire gravity of the film from sophomoric comedy to near-tragedy (anticipated by Karen's weeping when she tried to call Anders and Stoffer pointing to her belly). Karen is sitting in an alcove in the house, looking out into the garden, and is joined by Susanne. The backlighting from outside sometimes whitens the window panes; the faces, Susanne's especially, are shadowed in darkness.

Karen: 'We're so happy here. I have no right to be so happy.' Susanne: 'Oh, you have.' Karen shakes her head, weeping. Susanne, her eyes brimming and caressing Karen's tearful cheek: 'Of course you have. You're allowed to be here and you're allowed to be happy. Do you believe me?' Karen: 'Yes.'

Karen riding a
carriage alone

Susanne feeds
Stoffer

Karen responds to
Stoffer's greeting

Karen's dismay

Karen cannot make
the phone call

Spassing at the
swimming pool

Karen and Stoffer
debate

Jeppe's triumph

Karen's muted joy

Karen and
Susanne in the
pool

Katrine and Axel

Jeppe with the
bikers

The caviar
celebration

Stoffer out of
control

The orgy

Jeppe and
Josephine

Josephine's father
come to reclaim
his daughter

Jeppe's anguish

Stoffer intimidates
the group

Karen's farewell
speech

'I love you all more
than I have ever
loved anybody'

Anders' contempt
for his wife

Karen spasses

Susanne and
Karen depart

Two successive, and overlong, scenes of provocation follow. In midsummer the idiots are selling their horrible-looking Christmas ornaments assembled from the bits and pieces they've gathered in the forest. Whatever absurd price they quote, Ped, from his wheelchair, adds: 'And five pence.' A grimly tolerant neighbour grudgingly buys one.

Stoffer has a temper tantrum about the stupidity of the whole charade – presumably one he thought up – and throws the remaining decorations on the pavement. He then accosts another neighbour and accuses him of improperly maintaining his driveway cobblestones, causing the 'retards' to trip, and extorts him into buying all the remaining ornaments. Stoffer is still mad; Susanne shouts after him, 'Would you rather make kites?'

A well-heeled couple arrives to look at the house for sale; she does most of the talking. Gradually Stoffer explains that a home for the handicapped is just next door, and that the inmates like to come and visit; could they come now? The humour of the scene, such as it is, is based on the notion of the woman struggling to sustain her cheerfully tolerant attitude in the face of her growing horror at the situation, and her efforts to pretend that she and her husband are still interested when of course they aren't.

Fifth documentary: Henrik says the commune members were 'nice'. Off-camera, von Trier says that's odd, since the idea of pretending to be idiots didn't seem very 'polite'. Henrik recognises and considers the paradox.

The fake idiots, who aren't acting like idiots this time, have a luncheon lawn party for real idiots – i.e. people with Down's syndrome and the like. They are, of course, sweet and amenable. In the middle of the scene, back in the house, there is a brief moment in which Jeppe finds Josephine hunched over in fear; she asks to be left alone, but it's the first hint we get that she has had, or is having, actual psychological problems.

Back on the lawn, a real idiot is amused by a crooked fake-idiot Christmas ornament. Asked what she is doing there, Katrine says she's on holiday, which annoys Stoffer. He storms off angrily, complaining to Susanne that this is all 'sentimental crap', and outraged when she calls the real idiots 'cute' and when Henrik proposes to take a group photo. 'Hey, let's measure their skulls and gas them,' he responds. But Stoffer winds up taking the picture. One real idiot begins to sing, or croak. Katrine, or the actress playing her, Anne-Grethe Bjarup Riis, looks utterly disconcerted.

Sixth documentary: Ped says the group acted credibly as idiots. Henrik worries that maybe they sometimes went too far in their persistent provocations.

Everyone is morose. Nana mocks them for being flummoxed by the real idiots: 'They really got to you, didn't they?' She discovers Karen huddling in her alcove. Karen begins her first spass, mewling and squeaking. Everyone is so proud. Her mewling sounds carry over into the next scene (a technique von Trier uses frequently in other films, but not as often here). Karen and the others are back at the pool. Karen floats face up in the pool, crying and lovingly supported by Susanne and Jeppe. Axel is on the phone to his agency, which is pressuring him to return; he says he's still on paternity leave and that pool sounds in the background are a baby swimming class.

Axel at the house, in a jacket and tie, or 'dressed to kill', as he says in English. Katrine makes fun of him, but then capitulates to his charm, and off he goes to the agency; he has an important client to meet. Nana comes out and says to Katrine: 'You wade right into it, with both legs.'

Seventh documentary: Nana says Axel just wanted to fuck Katrine, 'four ways'. Axel, with wife to the side and baby on his lap, tries to articulate what von Trier reports Katrine has called his 'anti-middle-class' views, suggesting that those views might have something to do with the very idea of family. Axel's wife smiles with a kind of angry indulgence and the baby cries and is cuddled by Axel, who is reduced to platitudes. Nana says that Katrine did play a few harmless tricks on Axel, and is then seen back at the house helping her dress up.

At Axel's ad agency, he tries to explain to his utterly disbelieving boss that his slogan – 'child's food', meaning it's easy to handle, as he lamely tries to argue – for the account they're trying to wrest away from another agency is not complete drivel. Unfortunately, the company actually does make child's food, or baby food, which Axel hadn't known. But the boss is puzzled since the client, Benedikte, seems on the phone to be favourably disposed toward Axel. The boss says he's made up some 'flashy folders and charts and all – they're for another product and she won't look at them anyway'. Axel, rallying feebly, tries to convince the boss that his slogan is a sophisticated play on the company's product: the joke works better in Danish, since it's built on a word-play between the similar-sounding Danish words for 'baby food' and 'child's food'.

'Benedikte' arrives and it's Katrine, all dressed up. She is thrilled with the 'child's food' slogan, promising to commit a huge amount of the company's money towards it, but keeps slipping in and out of spass mode, to the boss's confusion and Axel's humiliation. Axel gets Katrine into a back room and only manages to get her to leave by giving her his credit card – which she uses to load up on champagne and caviar for a group feast.

Eighth documentary: Axel's wife tries to get him to admit that he fucked Katrine – that he 'humped the bitch', in the words of the subtitle. He won't admit it: 'That's not what it was all about.'

Stoffer leaves Jeppe in a bar/restaurant with three hulking, tattooed 'rockers', or bikers, in American parlance, and their girlfriend. Josephine worries that they might beat Jeppe up if they find out he's faking, but Stoffer says with typical hostility, 'He'll just have to play the part, then; it'll do him good.' Jeppe tries to leave, but the 'rockers' are sweet and solicitous, even helping him into the men's room and taking out his penis and running the water to encourage him and shaking his penis when he's finished. Stoffer returns and, out on the pavement, Jeppe runs off.

Back at the house, Karen tells Stoffer he was 'horrid' to Jeppe; Stoffer says Jeppe was just being a 'wimp', but grudgingly apologises. The group harmony steadily becoming more discordant, Stoffer and Axel offer competing claims as to who's the bigger bastard. The group settles down to the feast of champagne and caviar Katrine bought. It degenerates into an idiot game, with people smearing caviar on their faces. Karen is appalled at the waste. Karen: 'That's expensive stuff. There are people starving.' Stoffer: 'There aren't any people starving. That's the whole trick.' Karen clearly thinks she must flee, and borrows the phone again. She starts to dial, but then sees a man peering in the window.

He turns out to be a Søllerød city official, trying to bribe the commune into moving to a poorer neighbourhood. Miguel pretends to be Napoleon. Stoffer seems at first to be interested in the town's offer. Axel is discovered pissing on the man's car, which then needs to be jump-started. Things degenerate quickly, the idiots pretending to punish Axel with 'shock treatment' from the car. In a panic, the man backs his car down the driveway, jumper cables trailing behind.

Stoffer runs after him, screaming that he'll need police and dogs to get them out and that he's a 'Søllerød fascist'. But then, Stoffer starts having what seems be a real breakdown, peeling off his clothes and running hysterically down the suburban street. The group wrestles him, naked, to the ground and tries to carry him back to their van, but he keeps fighting and screaming about 'fucking fascists'. Neighbours look on horrified. Inside, everyone tries to get him upstairs, but he raves about being put in a 'padded cell'. Susanne (or someone; it's so dark it's hard to tell) says he's got to relax; that he's 'really zinging'. In the script, Ped suggests giving him a tranquillising injection. 'So you think I've gone really mad?' he asks. 'Are you scared now?' Finally, after a couple more outbursts, they tie him down and he goes to sleep.

The town official scene is the last one in the movie in which the group tries to provoke the bourgeoisie. But this time Stoffer's freak-out seems indeed to scare everyone; from now on, all their spassing, except for the very end, is done among themselves, and there's not much of it. The weight of the film shifts decisively toward the serious, the beautiful, the profound, the cruel, the terrifying and the cathartic.

Ninth and last documentary: Katrine truly misses her communal family, but realises that it's over and can never be reclaimed. Susanne says she was with Karen on the last day, and that she was the one who said goodbye to her, which implies, despite the abrupt ending, that when the two women leave Karen's parents' house at the end, they don't see each other again or even speak; what happens to Karen is never revealed.

The next morning Stoffer, seemingly chastened, comes downstairs to find everyone preparing for a party to celebrate his birthday – which it isn't but they seem to need a party. Stoffer: 'It's not my real birthday.'

Axel: 'Well, we're not real retards, are we?' As idiots, they enter a room (Jeppe tears the tickets, after some help; the room is festooned with Danish flags) and dance to recorded rock music.

Out of idiot mode, Susanne says Stoffer should choose what they do next. He chooses a 'gang-bang'. Susanne tries to dissuade him, and never really gets into it herself. Nana leads the way, saying she's always wanted a 'spasser fuck'. She lies naked on the floor and the others, back to being idiots, contemplate her bemusedly. But soon – with help from Nana reaching into Stoffer's pants – they're into it. Josephine wanders off, naked. Susanne holds back, but is chased into the garden and stripped down to her brassiere and boots, supposedly in good humour. Inside, the gang-bang is in full swing (although the only actual penetration shot was performed by two porn stars imported for the occasion). Karen sits on a windowsill, clothed and apart.

Upstairs, away from the action, Josephine stands naked against a wall. Jeppe, half-clothed, comes up the stairs. They begin an idiot love scene, tenderly touching each other and nuzzling and, finally, with about the sweetest tease-in in movies, they kiss. But somewhere in the kissing, their idiocy seems to drop away. These are 'real' people (remember, they're actors) making real love. 'I love you,' says the 'real' Josephine, twice, and then dissolves into what we presume to be tears of joy, which makes her tranquillised 'he was all right' in the fourth documentary so sad.

More sadness to come, the longest scene in the movie and the first of two family-drama encounters; this one is cruel and painful, but even it pales before the final scene of the movie. Here, the group is having breakfast outdoors the next morning when a stranger walks up the driveway. He looks to be about 45, and is coolly, hiply dressed, with black jacket, white T-shirt and sunglasses. Josephine's father.

At first taciturn but correct, he sits down between Josephine and Stoffer, who, like Axel at the other end of the table, is sitting in a wheelchair, although not in idiot mode. Stoffer and the others try to engage the father in conversation, but quickly his distant hostility, cold and implacable, becomes overt, von Trier's camera shifting back and forth among the speakers. The entire scene consists of down shots, as if the viewer were peering down at children.

'I'm not interested in discussing what you do,' says the father, as a jet roars overhead, the first one we've heard. When Stoffer suggests he might see things differently if he understood them, his response is, 'In vino veritas' (or so it says in the subtitles; he doesn't actually use the Latin; an English translation of the French text would read: 'Yes, I know, wisdom comes from the mouths of children and drunks'. Someone, off-camera: 'Josephine is happy here.' Father, looking at his daughter, who is crying: 'It certainly looks like it.' Stoffer: 'That's because you're here. She was fine until you came, but then you came crashing in.' Josephine, crying: 'I am really happy here.'

The father has come to reclaim his daughter, which apparently he has the legal right to do (her age is never specified, but she looks young, or maybe it's because she's been committed into his care; there is no mention of a mother). For the father, the only issue is that Josephine is not taking her pills; he's found them unopened at home. Father: 'You're going through hell.' Josephine: 'I'm not ... I'm not. For the first time, I'm feeling really great.'

The table has been sitting in stunned silence, but now she and the group and Ped – whom the father refuses to believe is a doctor – all argue that she's never been happier and that she doesn't need the pills. But the father insists and Josephine, despite her initial protests, doesn't have the strength to resist him. Jeppe sits still, traumatised into inaction. Katrine shouts to her and the group to resist, but to no avail; the patriarchy is too strong. Josephine goes inside to get her things. Stoffer and Ped have an argument about the pills, about which Ped knew nothing but which he insists she evidently doesn't need. Josephine emerges and walks with her father down the driveway to his car, followed by an angry Katrine: 'If you'd really been a proper father, she'd have been all right today.'

As Stoffer struggles to justify his inaction – 'We can't force anyone to stay' – Jeppe suddenly springs to life, running down the driveway in pursuit. He grabs the hood of the car, hanging on desperately. The father honks and turns on the wipers and tries to shake him loose; Josephine reaches out toward Jeppe from inside the car. 'You're insane,' screams Katrine, to the man who says he's taking away his daughter because she's insane. The group finally pulls Jeppe off the car, but he opens the passenger door and he and Josephine try to embrace, howling and screaming. It's truly a harrowing, primal scene. Finally the father drives off, leaving Jeppe sobbing on the ground, Stoffer and Katrine having a shoving match and the others seeking vainly to console the inconsolable Jeppe.

Inside the house, Jeppe's howls in the distance, things are clearly unravelling. Stoffer, bitter, attacks Ped for using the whole communal experience merely as material for his doctorate, and Henrik for being a no-talent artist trying to experience emotional extremes for the good of his art – to become 'a teeny bit mad, but not too much, just enough to be a proper artist'. Katrine accuses Stoffer of inaction in failing to prevent Josephine's departure, and says the others spass as effectively as he does.

Stoffer responds that he has no faith in them, and that the only way for them to prove their sincerity would be to spass in front of their family or at work. They play spin the bottle to determine who goes first. The bottle points to Axel, but he can't do it and leaves. The bottle's next choice is Henrik, who agrees to spass at his art class.

Suddenly we're in that class, full of elderly women who are thrilled to welcome him back. He begins an earnest lecture about Matisse or, as an increasingly disgusted Stoffer puts it, 'about a French faggot and his calligraphy'. Stoffer walks out noisily, and at the end of the class we learn that Henrik couldn't bring himself to spass in front of women who clearly admired him. 'I had no pride in my inner idiot,' he admits. 'I wasn't good enough.' He decides not to go back with the others. The lighting is so contrasted that most people look like backlit shadows.

At the Søllerød house, everyone is packing up; the experiment has failed. 'Let them go, Karen,' says Stoffer, slumped on the floor. 'It was all a lie.' But Karen wants to talk to the group, to embark on a course of action that will against all odds prove that Stoffer's self-indulgent spoiled-brat experiment wasn't a lie.

'I just want to say how happy I have been here,' she tells them. 'Being an idiot with you is one of the best things I've ever done.' She goes through them all lovingly, or all who are left (except for Stoffer), and blesses them each with kind words: Jeppe, 'who is almost like a little child I might have had'; Nana, 'who is so sweet and funny'; Miguel, 'who has such lovely eyes'; Ped, 'who is such a clever man'; 'strong, strong Katrine'. Again, most faces are in darkness, though most of them seem to be sniffling, certainly Karen, who is crying openly. Last, there is 'Susanne, who smiles at everyone so that the very heavens shine down on us. I believe … I love you all more than I have ever loved anybody … Maybe with one exception. But that was so long ago now.'

There is banging and sanding in the background; maybe someone has been called in to fix Axel's broken shed windows. Karen then says she wants to try spassing in front of her family tomorrow, Saturday: 'It is my turn to go home and see if I can be an idiot there.' It won't be pleasant, she adds, and asks – since the living room is too small to accommodate them all – that Susanne accompany her. Susanne agrees. 'I'd like that. Good,' says Karen. 'We'll see if I can show you it has been worthwhile.'

Instant cut to the outside of Karen's parents' front door, for the last and most terrifying scene of this or almost any film. There is no wasted dialogue, no music, not even the melodica; everything is cut surgically to the bone; much of the scene passes in pained silence, except for the insistent ticking of a clock. Karen's mother opens the door, surprised in a dulled way to see her, as is everyone they encounter inside. Her elder sister says they thought Karen was dead. No one embraces her; her younger sister asks her, 'What do you want?' This is the cold, cold Lutheran Scandinavian family of one's, or Ingmar Bergman's, nightmares, yet no one is caricatured; they are all just frozen with grief.

In the kitchen Susanne and we learn for the very first time that Karen's baby boy Martin died two weeks before and that she fled. The elder sister says she thinks the boy's death 'hurt Anders the most, what with her just disappearing and not attending the funeral'. Susanne is shocked.

Everyone inside – Karen's mother, her sisters; not so much her sedentary grandfather but especially her husband Anders, when he arrives – greets her with distant hostility. In a back hall Susanne finds Karen weeping over a photo of her dead baby; the red flowers on the bedsheet look like splattered blood. Susanne comforts and fortifies her. In the living room, Anders and the family sit stock still and silent, locked into their rigid grief. No spassing will save them. Karen ventures a halting apology for not attending Martin's funeral. Anders responds: 'It just means you aren't too upset. That's fine.'

Karen squeezes between Anders' chair and a lamp and into a couch seat next to her husband; Susanne is on another couch. Shot from Susanne's point of view, Karen begins to eat her cake. It comes oozing and foaming back out of her mouth, her head twisting sharply upwards and to the right. Anders hits her, hard, on the face. The family sits, locked; the clock ticks. Susanne looks on appalled and complicit; you can see her mind racing, trying to comprehend all this horror.

Karen continues to spass; she can't stop. It's like vomiting on her family. Susanne says: 'That's enough now, Karen.' Silence, ticking, coffee and blood dribbling down the left side of Karen's face. 'Shall we go?' Silence. Karen smiles tentatively. 'Yes.' Karen takes her hand, they walk out of the room, and the screen snaps dark, as if a light switch has been turned off.

Credits, including, Hollywood-comedy fashion, cute outtakes. Von Trier's name is not mentioned, according to Dogma rules.

## 2 Dogma Essence

*The Idiots* is a deliberate working out, refutation of and commentary on the points contained in the Dogma 95 manifesto (reprinted in this book's appendix). Von Trier read the manifesto at the Odéon theatre in Paris, birthplace of the 1968 student rebellion and shrine to nose-thumbing Euro-intellection, and then showered his audience with leaflets. *The Idiots* was intended to give life to theory.

The prose of the manifesto is overtly, parodistically French, with its street rhetoric and constant invocations of the New Wave. Shades of Godard, *Cahiers du Cinéma* and endless earnest cinematic manifestos. The French love manifestos, and so does von Trier. Inspired by Bergman, he prefaced what he calls his first trilogy of genre studies about Europe – *The Element of Crime* (1984), *Epidemic* (1987) and *Europa* (1991, also known

Dogma artifacts

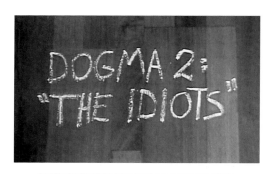

as *Zentropa*) – with a manifesto, and nearly every film since has been blessed with one as well. Manifestos are a way of clearing your conceptual throat, of staking your place in history and girding your filmic fantasies with intellectual substance.

France suffuses the opening of *The Idiots*. The melodica tune (or an electronic keyboard rigged to sound like a melodica and played live during the takes, as a shot in *The Humiliated* suggests) that makes its debut in the first sideshow scene – there is something Gallic about that scene's circusy ambience, too – is Saint-Saëns' 'The Swan', from his *Carnival of the Animals*. It was chosen (after some typical Trierian indecision) for its supposedly 'homosexual side', as per his journal, but it really serves to lend the whole opening scene and those afterwards in which it recurs a Truffaut-like wistfulness. Godard sent a fax approving of the film. '*The Idiots* is a modern film,' von Trier told Stig Björkman, 'but it is nevertheless nostalgic. It expresses a longing for the French New Wave and all its repercussions.'

Of course the revolutionary rhetoric is a self-conscious sham. The Dogma brotherhood had no intention of abolishing film-as-we-know-it. And the contrast between Hollywood gigantism and European low-budget simplicity was in place long before it was articulated (capitalised on?) here. Ditto the video revolution, although that had barely begun in early 1995 and entered into the Dogma methodology almost by accident. Leaders attract followers who already want to follow; they just need someone to articulate a goal.

But the idea of pruning the dead wood and excess, of calling upon film-makers (in Europe and independents everywhere and eventually in Hollywood itself) to strip away spectacle and technical frippery and concentrate on character and raw image – that was salutary. A sharp corrective to bloat is a common occurrence: it happened in the mid-1970s when English art- and arena-rock was supplanted by punk and what the guitarist Robert Fripp famously called 'small mobile intelligent units'.

In positing a 'technological storm' that will lead to 'the ultimate democratisation of cinema', the Dogma manifesto makes considerable sense. As technology becomes both increasingly sophisticated and available, more and more people can use it to undercut the authority of the elite. That's what happened in rock 'n' roll: cheap synthesisers and guitars and amplification allowed scrawny kids to fill arenas. Or the undermining of the record industry when more and more young people gained access to MP3 and other file-sharing computer technologies. Such revolutions are often led by a fringe that seizes the centre. Hence the tongue-in-cheek reminder of the military connotations of the term avant-garde. And hence the paradox of von Trier the rebel making a movie with Hollywood stars seems less of a paradox after all.

According to Jack Stevenson's study of von Trier, it was he who initiated the Dogma movement by calling up his friend Thomas Vinterberg one day in early 1995 and floating the idea. (Although it was Vinterberg who came out with the first Dogma film, *Celebration*; *The Idiots* is officially 'Dogma 2'.) Von Trier signs the manifesto on the Dogma website, and he and Vinterberg co-signed it on 13 March 1995. The other two Dogma 'brothers', Søren Kragh-Jacobsen and Kristian Levring, clearly played a lesser role in the creation of the manifesto, however fine *Mifune* and *The King Is Alive* may be.

So *The Idiots*, conceived at the same time as the manifesto, becomes among many other things von Trier's practical demonstration/confrontation with the rules he made up and then imposed on himself. 'I think Lars is the one who got closest to the essence of Dogma,' Bodil Jørgensen told the British critic Richard Kelly.

Dogma offers an enormous liberation, not just to directors but to actors as well. In his journal and in interviews von Trier has revelled in that freedom: the freedom to work quickly, to do his own camerawork, to shoot extended takes and then reshoot them without fretting about cost or continuity, to let actors act together and not just move cautiously to marks or in front of a blue screen.

The most interesting early modification of the Dogma rules came with the realisation that video could enhance that freedom. Dogma's Vow of Chastity insists that the 'film format must be Academy 35 mm', a bow to the 1:33 ratio of early silent cinema and hence a refutation of wide-screen Hollywood. Von Trier, who used a hand-held Steadicam for much of *Breaking the Waves*, resisted video. But even he recognised its flexibility and practicality, not to speak of economy, since video cassettes can run uninterruptedly for far longer than film. Vinterberg figured out the sophistic solution: Interpret Rule 9 to mean that the distribution format must be 35 mm film, no matter how the film is shot. That evasion allowed for von Trier's shooting most of *The Idiots* himself and for the intense ensemble work he drew from his actors.

It was no accident that the cast was recruited largely from the theatre. Theatre actors working on a Dogma film must feel right at home. They can work improvisationally, stretching out scenes until they snap. As he describes it in his journal, von Trier could massage scenes over and over – often in the process reducing speech and actorly acting to the barest of minimums – and not worry about cost. 'On *The Idiots* we had so many hours to play with,' said Jørgensen. 'You could go deeper and deeper into the mood of the scene, or in and out of the mood within the same take.'

This liberation of acting, whether or not a director chooses to follow Dogma rules strictly, has been often noted. Lone Scherfig, a part of the Filmbyen scene outside Copenhagen that also houses Zentropa, and whose Dogma film *Italian for Beginners* was much seen and praised, told *The New York Times*: 'This kind of film is very good for actors because there is so much focus on the acting. It reminds you of doing a play. You do the scene over and over again, and the camera just follows you. It was like playing a little scene on stage every time we did it.' In a *Hollywood Reporter* interview Jennifer Jason Leigh, who was in *The King Is Alive* and who subsequently co-directed the Dogma-esque *Anniversary Party* with Alan Cumming, said that Dogma 'makes for a very freeing kind of experience. You see how much you can get done. There's no energy wasted, no downtime; it keeps acting fresh and alive and fluid.'

It might seem a paradox that a manifesto intended to liberate comes freighted with what von Trier at one point in his journal jokingly calls 'these fucking Dogma rules'. No doubt that's why each Dogma director goes the whole hog just once and then picks and chooses among these and other techniques for subsequent films.

As he often does – years of therapy have some advantages – von Trier goes back into his past to explain the seeming paradox. Like so many children of the 1960s and 1970s (he was born in 1956), von Trier was raised permissively. His parents were left-wingers, and nudists to boot (though other relatives pushed that further, one of them refusing to wear clothes at home). Von Trier spent years in therapy in part to exorcise the influence of what he feared was an all-consuming mother. In revenge, he has argued, he and his generation needed to set rules. Von Trier pushed it further: he converted to Catholicism, to the horror of his parents. The ultimate source of dogma.

And he made *The Idiots*. He says it's the only film of his that his family ever liked. If so, that's a pretty sad comment on their artistic perspicacity, since in the end Stoffer and his group are revealed to be failures; for all their rationalist anti-rationalism they are redeemed only by the pure feeling of Karen. 'For me, rationalism is based on anguish,' von Trier told Björkman. 'If one fears chaos and if one hesitates to embrace life with all its conflicts and contradictions, one uses reason like a weapon. I have reacted like that myself, because of my past. In my family, everything was considered under the light of reason.'

Dogma rules and the difficulties even their creators have in following them led to an amusing shift in Dogma 95 procedure. Formerly, film-makers submitted their films and they were approved and certified by the brotherhood. But, says von Trier now, it's on the honour system: film-makers simply attest that they have followed the rules. 'Now it's more Protestant than Catholic,' he told me. 'They have to judge themselves. Before, it became a sport to cheat.'

If the Dogma brotherhood (and their brothers and sisters who make up the Filmbyen/Zentropa film complex started by von Trier and his principal producing partner Peter Aalbæk Jensen) is a sort of cell determined to infect the corpus of film, a metaphor for both communism and the cancers of von Trier's constant fears (see *Epidemic*), then the same might be said of Danish film itself. Denmark is that little country perched to the north of Germany, whose language no one else can speak and whose economic and military power is so puny that the only way to make a dent in the indifferent armour of the world is with the bacillus of culture. Why one country (in film: Italy in the 1950s, France in the 1960s, Iran and

Denmark now) springs to the fore at any time in any art is an accident and a mystery, of course: look at the plethora of first-rate operas coming out of Finland. But these seemingly sudden outbreaks have their causes.

In Denmark, there was Carl Theodor Dreyer, to whom von Trier has made conscious allusion (directing an unshot Dreyer script in his powerful 1988 television film *Medea*; likening the final family scene in *The Idiots* to something out of Dreyer). Von Trier is himself a boiling pot of cinematic self-consciousness, or better put, homages, since they rarely seem intrusive. And not just film: he calls Karen's summoning up of the will to leave her family at the end of *The Idiots* 'a real Nora moment'. For him, the forest scene in *The Idiots*, with the group cavorting amid the greenery, recalls Fellini and Truffaut (especially *Fahrenheit 451*); the references to Tarkovsky and

Echoes of *Fahrenheit 451* (François Truffaut / Anglo-Enterprises Film Productions, 1966)

Widerberg are many; and Bergman, whom he calls his 'spiritual father', is ever present – particularly in the alcove scene in which Susanne gives Karen permission to be happy, which reminds him (and us) of *Persona*. But how does filmic awareness, a constant checking of himself in the mirror of the pantheon, correlate with artless filmic innocence, as per Dogma?

If the Dogma manifesto reads like a Euro-rant against Hollywood, it might also seem an effort to liberate European films, and especially von Trier's own films, from their own past. The previous trilogy of *The Element of Crime*, *Epidemic* and *Europa* was a kind of study in the very genre films Dogma seeks to repudiate. *The Element of Crime* is a film noir of the noirest (or washed-out beigest) sort, *Epidemic* a kind of intellectual horror film, and *Europa* a historical political thriller.

Echoes of *Persona* (Ingmar Bergman / Svensk Filmindustri, 1966)

Of course von Trier's early work was far more than that, far more than the cheap genre studies attacked in the Dogma manifesto. All his life, and certainly from his student days at the Danish Film School (itself a source of the current Danish renaissance, along with government subsidies), his creativity was famously fecund. Even the television commercials he dismisses now – and gleefully skewers in the scene with Axel and Katrine at his ad agency – were wildly creative. There was the one in 1986 with naked women in a sauna and a man draping a newspaper over his erect penis; a foreshadowing of the shower scene in *The Idiots*, no doubt, with Stoffer getting his own erection. The commercial was a big hit in Denmark, but unaccountably did not get much international distribution.

The dark horse in the von Trier canon is *The Kingdom*, a television series set in a haunted hospital. Four hour-plus episodes were released in 1994, and another four came out in 1997 (since then, four of the principal actors have died, making a third series unlikely). This was a wonderful, Lynchian blend of horror and satire, grotesque happenings, soulful spiritualists and wild comedy. Not much in the way of exploited actresses or kinky eroticism here – though there was a bit of that – but a burst of liberating cinematic energy. The series has become a genuine cult hit on video, and rightly so. You can't understand von Trier's darker side without understanding this, which for all its ostensible terror has an irrepressible, almost Mozartean goofiness. Soap-operatic.

The Dogma manifesto and its Vow of Chastity were born of the same impulse that led to *The Idiots*. Apparently *La Grande Bouffe* (1973) and a Danish film, *Weekend* (1962, the first Danish film to emulate the French New Wave), served as initial inspirations for von Trier. But surely, one might think, the slightly parodistic anti-bourgeois 1960s tone of the manifesto is reflected in the earnest efforts of the idiots to *épater les bourgeois*. Of course, for all his personal and artistic adventures, Lars von Trier, with his film production business and second wife and four children and suburban house, has not exactly rejected bourgeois values himself. Just like Axel.

But perhaps this is not quite as hypocritical as it might seem. Stevenson, who wrote the first English-language book on von Trier, is

English but has lived in Denmark for many years. He offers an interesting digression on the Danish concept of 'the group', which he calls 'the cornerstone of modern Danish identity'. Apparently Danes regard communes differently from how Americans viewed them in the 1960s. They aren't so much refuges from society as monastery-like microcosms of society. Many Danes join groups for a while in their twenties, Stevenson says, their quest being 'as much an inner journey as any kind of outward rebellion'. Thus, he concludes, one can no more assume that Stoffer's motivation was simply to shock the bourgeoisie than that von Trier's, in creating Dogma, was to shock the film world.

In *The Idiots*, Stoffer certainly seems to be trying to shock and offend. But however highly one rates the level of provocation in either case, calling this movie, and implicitly the Dogma brotherhood, *The Idiots* undercuts the polemic, Dostoevsky references notwithstanding. The parallels between the Dogma brotherhood itself and the on-screen communards, and between the communard characters and the tight, sometimes incestuous acting ensemble documented in such detail in the journal, are obvious.

And the ironic parallels between the failed idealism, cruelty and petulance of Stoffer in the film and von Trier on the set were very deliberate. In *The Humiliated*, Jergil goes out of his way to stress the decline of Stoffer's grip on the commune as he senses the failure of his grand scheme and von Trier's dark nights of pessimism and despair as the filming draws to a close.

'This similarity between me and Stoffer in the film is becoming more and more glaring and grotesque,' von Trier writes in the journal, 'aside from the fact that Stoffer's infantilism is nothing next to mine.' During the editing he watches a television programme about Hitler and broadens the comparison to include him, 'that poor infantile spirit who tried to present in Europe his gigantic work of conceptual art'. Shades of Karlheinz Stockhausen and his ill-received comparison of the 9–11 terrorist attack with great art.

In that light, the role of Josephine's father takes on new meaning. Stoffer is the group leader, but he is powerless to stop the father (interestingly portrayed as a cool, stylish hipster) taking Josephine away, and this just after her tender love scene with Jeppe. Outside our little playpens, our little bands of Dogma brothers or communards or film teams or acting-out idiots, lies the real world, the world of paternal authority and money and institutionalised power. Commune inwardly or *épater* all you want, but in the end you'll be forced into the conformist mould.

And what about Dogma's Vow of Chastity, its now-famous set of ten inviolable rules? The very idea of chaste film directors is pretty funny. Movies are full of sex, and so are movie sets. Stars peddle sex; directors exploit it. The greatest sinners dream of abstention: witness des Grieux, fleeing as a priest to Saint-Sulpice but failing to escape the allure of the courtesan Manon Lescaut. Lars von Trier's early films were full of nudity and sex and eroticism; so are *The Idiots* and the films that preceded and followed it in the trilogy, *Breaking the Waves* especially. The very level of extreme emotion he elicits from actresses has been called erotic, and even likened to rape – of the characters (as with Bess in *Breaking the Waves*), of the women who act them and of the audience that is (von Trier's detractors fear) forced to watch them, to open themselves up to them.

Dogma's complaint against 'predictability (dramaturgy)', apart from the odd linkage of those two terms, seems hard to sustain. Dogma seeks reality, authenticity, over art (artifice). No more illusions. But that leads down a path where the barriers between art and life must crumble. Which in turn caused tensions before and after *The Idiots* shoot, and the bitter alienation between von Trier and Björk, who loved Selma and 'acted' (lived?) her from the heart and didn't want to see her suffer and die. Von Trier says he burst into tears when writing the death of Bess, so much did he love her, provoking a bitter outburst from his first wife about his ability to love his characters but not his family. Von Trier called Björk crazy; Björk called von Trier sadistic.

*The Idiots* is a film full of improvisation, which von Trier says led him and the actors away from the script and then largely back to it. It successfully opens up the acting and allows the actors to shape their characters, with von Trier following along like a puppy, pointing his camera (not framing; he makes the distinction) and taking it all in.

Yet especially on repeated viewings, the authorial hand, the dramaturgical mind, is everywhere evident. This is a film predicated on its surprise ending. We have no way of knowing that when Karen goes home to spass, her baby son has died. On a first viewing, the news comes as an extraordinary shock, a rollercoaster descent into personal tragedy whose final destination you cannot conceive. Where is von Trier leading us, his fascinated if horrified public?

But seeing the film again and again, you realise how carefully he has set up that surprise ending. Twice Karen tries to call home, then hangs up when she first gets an answer and then doesn't finally attempt the call. In the forest, Stoffer's pointing to her belly and wondering if it contains 'a little idiot who wants to come out' is painful when you know what has just happened, and obviously foreshadows the final scene. Right before that scene, when Karen makes her farewell speech to the group, by now bitter and alienated, she calls Jeppe the little child she might have had and ends by saying, 'I love you all more than I have ever loved anybody … Maybe with one exception, but that was so long ago now.' Contrasting with the antics of the idiots is Karen's sorrowful questioning and this authentic well of sadness emanating from her. It has to be heading somewhere, you realise, and where it's heading is home. This is not chance, a director taking down the improvisations of his actors. This is a plot, this is a script, this is dramaturgy, this is art.

Dogma is against illusion, against cosmetics. And truly, *The Idiots* is a rough film: the framing and sound can be ragged, the lighting varies from scene to scene, booms and even cameras crop up in shots, some characters (even after the massaging of the script during the shooting) are woefully underdeveloped, Miguel (Manuel in the script) especially, and continuity can be haphazard. The final scene, the scene in which Anders hits Karen in the face, was shot twice, and the second time a plate broke and cut Jørgensen near the left eye ('Dogma blood!' von Trier shouted joyfully, filming furiously before the actress was stitched up). In the final edit, the wound by her eye crops up in some shots and not in others.

But winnowing 130 hours of tape down to a 114-minute movie represents the imposition of art onto the raw energies of nature. And a particularly deliberate kind of art, one that mimics Dogma austerity through deliberate artistic choices. The editing is tight to the point of minimalism; scenes go by with hardly any dialogue, often in extreme close-up when the emotion becomes intense. After a scene is over, it's over, cutting abruptly to the next scene (or to a blank screen at the end). No wonder von Trier worried at one point that the film seemed slick and cold, and decided to use the documentary inserts as a leavening device, recalling a de-politicised *La Chinoise*. The inserts add their own layer of Dogma vérité to the mix.

As far as von Trier's adherence to the ten Vows of Chastity themselves is concerned, he wiggled and stretched – all recounted in tireless detail in the journal – but clearly not enough to deny himself a Dogma certificate.

Some of the minor violations of the rules were inadvertent on von Trier's part. Recent prints of the film forswear forbidden optional filters, for instance, but Vinterberg dressed von Trier down when he discovered that 147 filters had indeed been used in the film's first prints to alleviate excessive darkness. Von Trier says they were snuck in by Peter Aalbæk Jensen and another key Zentropa producer, Vibeke Windeløv, without his knowledge ('The labs live on that,' he told me). Now, he adds, a Dogma loyalist forever, that the film looks better without them, although many scenes are indeed so dark that the characters seem like silhouettes.

In sticking to a ban on 'temporal and geographical alienation', von Trier shot the film more or less in order over the two-week span of the plot. He tried his best to create a bonding of the actors comparable to the bonding of the characters. He eagerly exploited every life–art parallel he could uncover, including the severe illness of Bodil Jørgensen's own little son, who underwent a heart operation and then, on the eve of the alcove scene, came down with a temperature of more than 105 degrees.

He failed in nearly every one of his attempted actor–reality parallels, however, not least because he failed to get the actors to actually live communally in the big, empty house that served as the set. There were clashes, particularly bitter ones between von Trier and Knud Romer Jørgensen, who played Axel. And the bitterness persisted after filming was completed. Some of the cast felt betrayed by the revelations in von Trier's *Intimate Journal*. In 2002 Denmark's Actors' Union actually sued Zentropa on behalf of the cast, claiming they had not received their rightful royalties. (Zentropa argued that the complexity of the deal cobbled together to raise the $3 million needed for the film guaranteed the Dutch and French co-producers first rights to the limited box-office take.)

Genre films, against which Dogma declares war, are everywhere among us, including the genre of the ragged avant-garde film made communally on the cheap. Von Trier himself is a master of genre, as in his first trilogy. Even his recent films thrive on the clash of genres. *The Idiots* starts out as a supposedly rude comedy, even though some of the scenes that von Trier in his journal finds hilarious might strike others as queasy. A few of the putatively comic scenes actually are funny, to be sure, although always with an edge: above all the one where Katrine embarrasses Axel by spassing in his ad agency, the craven executives trying their best to ignore the antics of the all-powerful client.

But there is more, and of course von Trier knew it all along. 'I tried to imbue [this film] with life and lightness, and I've succeeded,' he told Peter Øvig Knudsen, who transcribed the journal tapes, in an interview on the Dogma website. 'Some people say it's all very silly, and yes, that is exactly what it is. But the film contains other facets.'

From the first scene of the film there is Karen's weighty, childlike sadness, carrying her terrible secret. You can't call this movie a comedy – despite the desperate, cheesy efforts of the designers of the video cassette in America. 'Take a long ride on a short bus,' the package copy nonsensically burbles, accompanying a cartoon of a kind of Ken Kesey bus of happy, happy idiots. Likewise the cover of the British DVD, which singles out a frame of three naked idiots running across a lawn, thus carefully excising any notion that this might be a profound, nearly tragic, harrowingly emotional journey.

Looked at another way, the film is a tragedy that ends in weird triumph. But you can't just discount the communal shenanigans; they form the necessary dialectical context, the punk rock contrast to Karen's operatic grief. So, far from repudiating genre conventions, *The Idiots* thrives on them. So does *Dancer in the Dark*, which von Trier describes as a deliberate attempt to undercut the happy-ending aura of the old-fashioned musical (particularly *The Sound of Music*, which recurs throughout) with what he calls 'melodrama'. But *Dancer in the Dark* is not a Dogma movie.

Von Trier has argued to me that in the extreme, which is where he wants to go, humour and tragedy become one. 'When we were writing scripts that don't have humour, we were laughing all the time; we had such a good time. I like things on the edge, but it can be tragic or humorous.'

Dogma's notion of an uncredited director is a pure conceit, of course, in that no one is more of an auteur than Lars von Trier, and no one who cares doesn't know who directed which Dogma film. Indeed, von Trier almost boasts in his journal of the film as an exorcism of his lonely youth, slumping on the sidelines of parties where everybody else had fun but now in triumphant control: 'This film compensates for the defeats of my youth in relation to the group. I feel that very strongly and it's very satisfying. I don't know if it's the power over the people that is so satisfying … but surely at least part of the satisfaction is that this is my game for me that we're playing.'

Dogma forswears bourgeois good taste. Von Trier certainly went a long way to 'force the truth' out of his characters. He certainly transgressed the bounds of good taste, in the initial conception of the film (normal people playing at being retarded) and in innumerable scenes throughout, above all the encounter (of the characters and the actors who played them) with the actual Down's syndrome patients. Despite his enthusiasm for what he perceives as the hilarity in the scenes of awkward and embarrassing confrontation between the idiots and the bourgeoisie, and despite the real moral of the film, which is that Karen's authenticity of feeling both shows up the cruel shallowness of Stoffer's ideas and validates them, von Trier is keenly aware of the power of bad taste, bad manners, in a proper social situation. His attitude toward the communards is an uneasy mix of affection, disdain and wit.

Onlookers, bystanders, non-
professionals

Von Trier has cited Rudolf Steiner's notion of Mongolians as angels from heaven, but his actor-Mongolians often seem painfully self-indulgent (even after von Trier shot and reshot to encourage underplaying). Which they are supposed to be, but it makes for periodically uncomfortable viewing. The audience becomes one with the offended bourgeoisie.

When Karen spasses in front of her family, the cake and coffee dribbling from her mouth seems in that fraught context like the most violent betrayal of social codes. In his journal, von Trier writes that 'this little piece of cake that comes out of her mouth is a terrible transgression'.

But is all this 'beyond aesthetic considerations', as Dogma would have it? Of course not. *The Idiots* is a film about art (and authenticity) by a supreme artist. And ultimately, Dogma is itself a quixotic quest for authenticity, a kind of method acting liberation of the personal in the service of the artistic. Emotional force is supposed to be real, not artificial; felt, not acted. But von Trier constantly sought strategies to disorient and disconcert his actors, professionals all, presumably for the good of the film or their performances – or maybe, as we shall see, for his idea of what was good for them as people. His principal strategy – other than the psycho-therapeutic manoeuvres he undertakes – was the periodic introduction of non-professionals into the mix. In ascending order of confusion for the professionals, these include the cheerful old lady art students before whom Henrik tries and fails to spass, the 'rockers' who help Jeppe pee, the actual porn stars brought in for the penetration shot in the gang-bang, and, most disconcerting of all, the actual 'Mongolians' (so listed in the cast), who come for lunch, who seem to be having a lovely time, and who pose happily for a group photo. They don't, blessedly, get naked. (The extreme case in the von Trier œuvre of the introduction of a non-professional was the casting of Björk as Selma in *Dancer in the Dark* – which led to tension on the set, dazzling artistic success and bitter personal estrangement.)

At a point of euphoria in the journal, overwhelmed by his own talent (which of course leads immediately to a spasm of fear that he will be punished with cancer), he speaks contentedly of 'a day in the Trier puppet theatre'. This might seem demeaning to the actors, another proof that von

Trier still could not relate to actors as human beings and collaborators, but not necessarily. Puppets have magic. They're wooden, not alive, mere playthings. But they come to life, and that life can seem real; that's what Kleist was about; that's what Pinocchio is about. In her book *The Secret Life of Puppets*, Victoria Nelson circles back several times to von Trier. She doesn't say he uses his actors like puppets. She credits him with restoring a lost spirituality to a Western world which for centuries has suppressed those ancients truths.

Watching this film, reading the journal, considering *The Humiliated*, one is struck again and again how von Trier (and the actors, in their hours-long discussions) torture themselves (if that's the word – sometimes they thrill themselves) with their constant considerations of the borderlines between professional and amateur, normal and retarded, actor and character. What makes this film supreme, for all its miscalculations and awkwardnesses and out-of-tune moral tone, is this impassioned sincerity of acting. Maybe there was tension on the set and maybe von Trier crossed a line or two in seeking to draw out emotion from his actresses and maybe there have been tensions since the film came out. But watching *The Idiots*, you feel that these are people devoted not just to their careers, as von Trier laments in one moment of despair, but to the film and to the impossibly elusive goal of an acting so true that it obliterates the boundaries between life and art.

Which is just what Dogma 95 set out so boldly and foolishly and bravely to do.

# 3 Tears

We live bathed in tears, from the *Lamentations of Jeremiah* and the tears on the Madonna's cheek to the Lake of Tears in Bartók's opera *Bluebeard's Castle* to the Miracles' 'Tracks of My Tears' to the Palace of Tears, a conceptually inspired techno-disco in the grim Volkspolizei building in the former East Berlin. Christ pierced by a Roman spear; Justine writhing under the Marquis' lash.

Karen Durbin, a New York film critic who has written more perceptively about von Trier than anyone I know in any language I can read, once suggested that 'there is a monograph to be written on his sensuous use of water imagery'. What she's alluding to is the washed-out shots of Venetian canals in *The Element of Crime*, the most ominous evocation of Venice's death aura since Mann's *Death in Venice*; the disease-breeding marshes of *Epidemic*; the cold oceans and watery bogs of *Medea*; the dripping sub-basement pipes and ghostly fluidic emissions of *The Kingdom*; the all-surrounding sea, isolating Jan and forming a deadly passage to the rusty tanker that Bess must traverse, in the liquidly titled *Breaking the Waves*; and the swimming-pool scenes in *The Idiots*, especially when the slowly accepting Karen floats like a baby in amniotic fluid, supported by her new friends. Plus the tears that almost invariably course down the cheeks of von Trier's lead actresses, especially in the trilogy of which *The Idiots* is the arch-stone.

There were strong performances, and especially strong performances by women, in earlier von Trier films: one thinks of the implacable Kirsten Olsen as Medea or the conflicted, seductive Barbara Sukowa in *Europa* or the tremulous, Miss Marple-like amateur ghostbuster, Kirsten Rolffes, in *The Kingdom*.

But not counting *Dogville* and its sequels, and hence not counting Nicole Kidman, and not counting *The Idiots*, the two astonishing female performances in films by von Trier were by Emily Watson as Bess in *Breaking the Waves* and Björk as Selma in *Dancer in the Dark*. Plus their foils, their confidantes, their emotional mirrors, Katrin Cartlidge as Dodo in *Breaking the Waves* and both Cathérine Deneuve as Kathy and Siobhan Fallon as Brenda, the prison guard, in *Dancer in the Dark*.

Water imagery in *Element of Crime* (Per Holst Filmproduktion A/S, 1984),
*Breaking the Waves* (Zentropa Entertainments ApS, 1996) and *The Idiots*

What links these performances, and them to Karen and Susanne in *The Idiots*, is the enormous vulnerability of these women, and especially of their faces in extreme close-up. It's as if the barriers of actorly craft have fallen away, as if something almost unbearably real is confronting you unmediated from the screen. Wagner built a theory of opera about the union of words and music, the former representing the 'masculine', rational side (or side of the brain, as we'd say today), the latter the 'feminine' emotionality without which reason would seem dessicated. The faces of these film actresses, their unguarded luminosity, is like the music of an opera, girding the plots with an emotional depth without which mere words and characters and plot would seem impossibly superficial.

Watson, in her first film role, leaping in at the last minute for Helena Bonham-Carter, established her reputation as Bess, the child-woman who loves God so deeply she speaks with him daily and yet who twists her passion for her husband Jan and her grief in his incapacitation (including, of course, his sexual incapacitation) into a bizarre, masochistic need to abase herself for his salvation. Which miracle, of course, she achieves.

Björk is even more openly pained, helpless, noble against the betrayals inflicted upon her by everyone she knows and loves (except, maybe, for Fallon's kindly guard). In her songs and concerts and videos, Björk had already revealed a childlike well of feeling that set her far apart from most pop stars. But on film, she opens herself up so deeply that you fear for her sanity and her survival. It was, apparently, a justified fear. Her eyes well with tears, even in joy; a weeping sadness seems to define her soul.

Water and sexuality are inseparable; the floods of tears from Bess and Selma and Karen and Susanne are an erotic release, and the reason those tears move some critics to cry brutality and rape. Each actress brought something ineffable, something of her own, to her part. But von Trier cast them and directed them, and he worked hard to elicit those tears, using every trick in the director's and the therapist's book. His methods have been questioned; the line between collegial artistry, directorial authority (even in a Dogma film) and none-too-subtle sadism are, well, watery.

Weeping in *The Idiots* and
*Dancer in the Dark*
(Zentropa Entertainments
ApS, 2000)

But the profoundly moving, profoundly disturbing emotion he has
drawn from his actresses is art at its deepest level. Like an artist with his
models, he has shaped them into something greater than themselves and,
as male artists have always done, sometimes he has fallen into romantic or
erotic relationships with them.

In art and in life, beneath all the Euro-conceits of *The Idiots*, lies
emotion of the most primal sort, and Dogma techniques – the fluid
camera movements, the improvisational acting, the close-ups, the
*cinéma vérité* crudeness of the camerawork, the illusion or actuality of
things on the screen being 'real' – all contribute to that emotion. The
absence of music: this kind of erotic female emotional release makes a
music of its own.

# 4 The Artist and His Models

'He's a unique eccentric, and he's very proud of that,' said Watson in a 2002 London *Times* interview.

Also, he has a dangerous intelligence where there's too much going on in his head for the life he has or something. But it's wonderful to be around, it's very intoxicating. I think I'd love to work with him again when he's moved on from his 'women having a bad time' stage. I'm sure he will.

'I'm very excited for Nicole,' said fellow Australian Russell Crowe about Nicole Kidman's Oscar nomination for *Moulin Rouge* (2001), as reported in *Daily Variety*. 'She's in Sweden with Lars von Trier, so I know she's had a bad day. The nomination will probably make her feel a lot better.'

'Acting is extreme cruelty, or *this* acting was,' said Björk – the woman von Trier now refers to as 'this Icelandic lady' – on Charlie Rose's highbrow American television chat show.

I think creativity doesn't have to be cruel to be good. I think it's a sign of impotency if you think you have to add cruelty to your work for it to be considered art. I think if you are confident in your art, you would just nurture it with positive energy.

At least until his *Golden Heart* trilogy in the 1990s, von Trier had a perhaps deserved reputation as a director who was uncomfortable directing actors. In his youthfully arrogant view, he was the director, the auteur. He had written the scripts, and it was the actors' job to toe the line, unquestioningly.

'For me, it's an indication of professionalism that actors follow the director's instructions,' he told a newspaper interviewer in 1984, as cited in Stevenson. 'It's his vision ... Danish actors ... demand to "understand" their roles. But what is there to understand if the director knows precisely what he must have?'

Such an attitude hardly endeared him to actors, or actresses. Even in the 1990s, in *The Kingdom*, he turned over much of the direction of the actors to a frequent assistant, Morten Arnfred. At a press conference as late as 1997, after the first screening of the second series of *Kingdom* instalments, the actress Kirsten Rolffes stated: 'Lars von Trier cannot direct actors.' Especially women actors, and one reason was that he either fought them or fell in love with them. By his own account, in his *Idiots* journal,

At the beginning of my career I had a very complicated relationship with actresses … I was practically on a war footing with them and they always pretended they had no confidence in me, or I never felt they had confidence in me; they were convinced that I was belittling them … yes, it was a mixture of anguish and rage.

And yet there are all those wonderful performances by women in his films, especially in the 1990s and even in *The Kingdom*. And it might seem a long way from absolutist auteurism to the making of *The Idiots*, with Danish actors given considerable latitude for improvisation and collaborative input. Had von Trier changed, and if so, how?

Despite manic bursts of elation – 'I'm too gifted, too gifted … but I'm too gifted,' from the journal – von Trier would never claim a sure grip on mental health. His panic attacks and phobias and obsessions and counteracting anti-depressants are so well known, mostly because he dwells on them in such detail, that (despite his four children) a proud boast of potency is unlikely to escape his lips. He won't fly or take a boat (other than his beloved kayak), and travels long distances only grudgingly by car. He has now shot two movies in Scandinavia that were supposedly set in the United States. At the height of his depression during the filming of *The Idiots*, as seen in *The Humiliated*, he looks like a little boy lost at his own party, thrown back despite himself into the loneliness and alienation of his childhood. This is a man who begins his *Idiots* journal with a discussion of the consistency of his shit, and twice tells us how he needs to masturbate five times a night to get to sleep, then commiserates with his abused penis.

Everyone is male and female, rational and sensual, brilliant and silly, good and bad, kind and cruel. We struggle to resolve these opposites within ourselves. Like so many artists, von Trier seems to have a more fraught set of dichotomies, and the dialectical resolution of that tension is a wellspring of his art.

And for all his earlier inability to communicate with actors and actresses, it is now the raw emotion he draws from his actresses, especially in the *Golden Heart* or Good Women trilogy of which *The Idiots* is the centrepiece, that has shocked and thrilled and horrified people, and defined his reputation. Durbin is a longtime feminist who is deeply sympathetic to von Trier and his relationships with actresses. But even she is forced to amazement at the controversy von Trier provokes, quite often deliberately.

Durbin tells the story of *Dancer in the Dark* at Cannes, and of 'two American critics and longtime friends' – both women – 'who argued so bitterly over the film that they didn't speak for the rest of the festival'. *The Idiots* has been included in lists of the most important films of the 1990s and dismissed by Alexander Walker in the London *Evening Standard* as a 'repugnant piece of offensive drivel'. *Dancer in the Dark* won the Palme d'or at Cannes but caused A. O. Scott, a *New York Times* critic, to portray the film as a battle between Björk's 'artistic conviction' and von Trier's 'aestheticized cynicism'. He also believes that the miraculous final scene of *The Idiots* 'descends to a truly contemptible emotional brutality'.

For von Trier, life seems to be a polarity between reason and feeling. In *The Idiots* that polarity plays out as a struggle between Dogma rules and the nose-thumbing, male-dominated idiot commune on the one side and the bottomless well of feeling represented by Karen and Susanne on the other. As we have seen, von Trier is not the first to identify reason with masculinity and emotion with femininity. In nature the cavorting communards are humanised and softened. They can let down their bristling urban, rationalist guard; they gain more naturalness and essence in the forest or the pool than any self-conscious search for an 'inner idiot' might bring them. It is no accident that von Trier, in the course of shooting, moved the moment in which Stoffer tries to explain his philosophy to a puzzled Karen from the house to the forest. All these tensions, his 'masculine' intellectual brilliance and assertiveness and raw ambition, his 'feminine' fears and isolation and deep wells of feeling, he translates directly into first his writing, then his directing and his relations to the actors.

Von Trier now says that all his films, with a male or female protagonist, tell a single story, and that all the characters are aspects of himself. 'It's the same story and the same theme as always,' he told me. 'It's the humanist and idealist who goes out into the world and finds there values that are *not* humanist or idealistic and then he fails. If it's a man or a woman, I don't think there's a lot of difference. How I write is to take my own character and divide it into different characters. I project myself into the male and the female.'

All his life (his whole life, not just his professional life) von Trier has been fascinated with sexuality, and mostly that sexuality is heterosexually expressed, hence a lot of female nudity and a lot of women placed in erotically compromising positions, psychologically and physically. For him, sex is not only fun (real sex, fantasy sex, voyeuristic sex, which is what you get looking through a camera), but it serves a higher purpose. Not just to shock the bourgeoisie, but to liberate the self from the strictures of reason and good taste.

Among *The Idiots*' cast members, the one with a particularly strong resistance to the nudity, it seems, was Trine Michelsen, who played the role of the hard-bitten outsider Nana, drawn to the group personally but cynically resistant to their spassing. Michelsen had had some soft-core porn experience, and it was her friendship with hard-core porn stars that enabled von Trier to find the actors he used in his orgy scene. Still, Michelsen – who does in fact appear fully and frankly naked in several of the film's scenes – constantly questioned her motivation for nudity. 'I had a long discussion with Trine, who fears that we use her only as a doll for getting undressed, and I think that's not true,' he writes at one point. But the journal also contains interesting speculations on how the role-playing of sex does and does not relate to the role-playing of actors.

During the shooting, he would hold periodic 'all naked days': supposedly not for titillation but for relaxation, harking back to his youth and his parents' interest in nudism. He argues in the journal that communal nudity is liberating in that it frees the mind from the seductiveness of clothed (sometimes barely, as in a bikini) sexuality. But he also regrets a certain prudery of the modern world: of the orgy scene, he told Björkman, 'I was naive enough to believe that the actors would wind up fucking together. They didn't do it. In the 60s, they would certainly have let themselves go … !'

His own excitable prurience sometimes undercuts his high-minded rationales for nudity. Still, he insists doggedly, not just nakedness but overt sexuality are 'not simply infantilism, as one might think. It's important for me because it gives the film a kind of roughness' – the word is in English and italics. He adds, interestingly, that 'we had besides a counsellor who works at the Ebberødgaard asylum, and who said that we had captured the handicapped well but we had slighted their sexuality … To make a film about the handicapped without taking that aspect into account is a little like Pietist literature about sex.'

Still, von Trier evinces a kind of adolescent excitement during some of his sex scenes. The script calls for Stoffer to have an erection during the shower after their first visit to the swimming pool. The actor, Jens Albinus, eventually managed one, but not before a good deal of trouble, which von Trier jokingly threatened to overcome with a mega-Viagra-style injection that would give him a two-hour hard-on. The director also gleefully reports 'a very active and positive intervention by Susanne' as part of the effort; in *The Humiliated* we see her on her knees, industrious with the lather. Of course, Susanne is the actress Anne Louise Hassing, the subject of von Trier's most super-heated fantasies.

Despite scenes in the film and entries in the journal that might indeed suggest an onanistic fascination with improvisational nudity and sex (as opposed to that dictated sternly by the script and Dogma rules), it is clear that von Trier loves his characters and, by and large, the actors who embody them. The actresses who played them loved them too; Björk loved Selma and bitterly resented von Trier for torturing and killing her. Despite his resentments toward his mother and his first wife, it would seem from the evidence on screen that von Trier does indeed love, admire and respect women; he certainly has surrounded himself with creatively 'empowered' women at Zentropa. The central figures' terrible deaths in *Breaking the Waves* and *Dancer in the Dark* come from some other place, some need to follow the implacable resolution of tragic consequences, and a belief that the death of these women will accomplish some redemptive good, as in Christian martyrdom.

Von Trier told Björkman that the genesis of *Breaking the Waves* (and the forthcoming trilogy) was

> a children's book called *Golden Heart* (a Danish fairytale) which I have a very strong and fond memory of. It was a picture book about a little girl who went out into the woods with pieces of bread and other things in her pocket. But at the end of the book, after she's passed through the woods, she stands naked and without anything. And the last sentence of the book was, '"I'll be fine anyway,"' said Golden Heart.' It expressed the role of the martyr in its most extreme form.

In fact, *Golden Heart* and its variants ostensibly end happily, with the heroine rewarded by a Prince or by God, a deus ex machina that von Trier omits. Peter Schepelern, a Danish writer who is perhaps the most detailed researcher of the von Trier œuvre, has come up in his book *Lars von Triers Film* with illustrations not only from *Golden Heart* but two other fairytales. There is the Swedish picture book, *Burre Busse i trollskogen* (*Burre Busse in the Troll Forest*), in which a naked little girl is surrounded by threatening pine trees with trolls' faces. And there is the Grimm Brothers' German fairytale 'Die Sterntaler' ('The Star Coin'), in which a similar little orphan, 'good and pious', gives away everything she has – she's modest enough to say to herself, as she divests herself of her last article of clothing, 'It is a dark night, nobody can see anything, you might as well give away your skirt' – and is rewarded with a shower of heavenly coins.

With or without a happy ending, the image of naked martyrdom runs deep in Germanic fairytales, which include the Danish and Swedish subsets. But it is also present, more darkly, in the Marquis de Sade, and it turns out that Sade's *Justine* was an equally important source for *Breaking the Waves* and the whole *Golden Heart* trilogy. *Breaking the Waves*, at the beginning of its gestation, was to be an erotic film. Justine, like Golden Heart, retains her purity throughout her indignities. But sexuality, like masochism, is also an act of giving, a surrender to one's deepest and maybe best instincts.

The vision of the thrill of capitulation has graduated from Sade and German Romanticism through Freud to the 1960s to today, albeit sideswiped not only by right-wing religiosity but also by the more puritanical forms of feminism. Feminist thought is divided on the issue of the free heterosexual expression of female sexuality, and even pornography, as salutary and liberating or demeaning and enslaving. Durbin, for one, is a pro-sex feminist, and though she seems amused at the thought that von Trier is a wickedly perverse 'little monster' (he's called himself a troll), she nonetheless has written that 'von Trier's work displays a singular sense of identification with women'.

Some might argue that even if he does identify with women, that merely suggests a level of self-hatred comparable to his hatred of his characters. But for me and, I would argue more polemically, for any fair-minded viewer, the depth and poignance of his recent female characters is so strong that they can only love, and be loved.

That does not mean, however, that they suffer the same fates, similarly tragic and horrible. Bess, who loves God and matrimonial sexuality in dangerously equal measure and offers herself up sacrificially for

Illustration by Ludwig Richter for 'Die Sterntaler'

her paralysed husband, undergoes a horrible gang rape and death, and is rewarded in heaven – quite literally: the final shot looks down from God's perspective at church bells and clouds with the husband's offshore oil rig far below. Those bells have been controversial, but have precedents in at least two von Trier student films featuring sacrifice and religious redemption. Von Trier today is unapologetic: 'That's what I mean about going all the way,' he told me. '*Of course* there should be bells there.' Selma seems a mute and helpless lamb, with all the Christ-like connotations of that word, but when she dies she has saved no one, let alone all mankind.

In von Trier's scripts each of these central women is shadowed by a sympathetic female double. Bess, Karen and Selma have a principal female ally whose comfort and support sustains them, or at least provides some solace on their stony path toward death. Bess has Dodo, Karen has Susanne, and Selma has a combination of Kathy (who is cut off from her when she is in prison and remains, like everyone else, unaware of her actual innocence) and Brenda, Siobhan Fallon's comforting prison guard, who steadies her in her final days. It is their sympathy, their intense, tearful, emotional bonding, that reinforces the emotional and sexual poignance of the central figures.

Nowhere is that more true than in *The Idiots*, with the characters of Karen and Susanne – as conceived by von Trier in his script; below we'll consider Bodil Jørgensen's and Anne Louise Hassing's performances, and von Trier's means of eliciting them. Stoffer is the leader of the group, but the dynamic in the film is between him and the outsider Karen. Karen's slow, quiet ascension and final vindication of the group's idiot philosophy – a vindication that Stoffer has singularly failed to achieve himself – makes the film into her triumph, not her tragedy. It earns that triumph through the most raw and painful and even horrific means, but the triumph is still real. Susanne, her compassionate, complicit shadow, was envisaged by von Trier as a childhood friend of Stoffer's and a nurse, although these biographical details have dropped out in the final film.

But how does von Trier move from page to screen with his female characters? Are his methods cruel, sadistic, manipulative, as his critics (and at least one of his actresses) charge? A simple answer is that directors (despite Dogma de-emphasis) are still masters of their ships, and 'twas ever so. Especially if they are also the writers, they are the true auteurs of the film. Like the conductor of an orchestra, they are the only ones who can see the interests of the whole, and encourage/cajole/terrify the other collaborators (musicians, actors) into the fullest possible realisation of that vision. Lots of famous and successful directors have been tyrants, beating brilliance from their actor-children.

Von Trier himself clings to the idea of professionalism in moments of crisis, despite its supposed slighting in the Dogma manifesto. In conversation with me he went so far as to say that Björk's real problem on the *Dancer in the Dark* set was that as a rock star/diva she resented being told to show up for work on time every morning. One suspects that should she choose to be more forthcoming about her complaints, they would be a little more psychologically nuanced than that. Stevenson, for one, argues that the entire relationship between von Trier and Björk put at least as much strain on him as on her.

But clearly von Trier does resort to extreme means and, like other directors, has developed complex, tortured relations with his actresses, which relations have not always profited the film. But it is hardly unprecedented that directors consort with their actresses, or artists with their models. Bergman, one of von Trier's idols, lived with Liv Ullman for four years and had a child with her.

Who, one might wonder, is being humiliated in *The Idiots* as documented in *The Humiliated*? Critics like Scott apparently think it's actresses like Jørgensen and Hassing. Karen might think it's the idiots, embarrassing themselves with their cruel and childish games. Von Trier seems to think it's himself. As shooting winds down, he slumps dejectedly into a conviction that his film is a failure and that only he ever had the slightest faith in it. 'One is 195 per cent alone in one's tiny little world, ridiculous and humiliating,' he whimpers.

Yet to ignore the sexuality of power and the dependency of those under a director's sway is naive. From the middle of the two-week shoot to the end, von Trier broods increasingly that he's shut out of the happy bonding of the actors. Of course he is; he's the director, and hence by definition detached, and beyond that he is by nature a 'distant person', according to Steen. It's not just that women (let's keep it simple; women can dominate men and there are male and female homosexual dependent relationships too) capitulate to men's sexual desires and psycho-sadistic demands because they want to keep their jobs. Power and powerlessness can be aphrodisiacs, for both sides. Teachers and students. Bill and Monica.

Von Trier spends considerable time fretting about these very issues in his *Idiots* 'intimate journal', largely as a result of his efforts to practise therapy on himself and come to terms with his obsession with Hassing. It was an obsession that included actions on von Trier's part that hurt and

Von Trier directs Emily Watson in *Breaking the Waves* (Stig Björkman, *Tranceformer*, AB Memfis Film & Television, 1997)

Von Trier and Björk at Cannes (© Film Four Ltd, 2000)

alienated the actress, shutting down her emotions just when von Trier needed them the most. In his view, far from wallowing in new levels of depraved cruelty, he has evolved from antagonism to complicity with his actresses, from which his fantasies about Hassing represented both a confirmation and a regression. But he concludes that if complicity includes fantasy or even an on-the-set affair, so be it.

He hastens to add that he knows his feelings are childish – 'I'm 12 years old again and shivering' – and thus tries to broaden his feelings beyond Hassing to include others, and not just women, as in the actor who plays Jeppe, Nikolaj Lie Kaas: 'Nikolaj, for example, it's impossible not to fall madly in love with him, albeit asexually,' he nervously adds. But he keeps coming back to Hassing, and he's furious with himself (his new wife was about to give birth to twin boys). 'It's just a stupid on-location love affair, it's too infantile,' he complains.

The real issue is between him as a director and the actresses who play the leading roles, and the secondary actresses, whether or not he has a crush on them. Did his behaviour with Watson and Jørgensen and Björk, and with Katrin Cartlidge (his obsession during the filming of *Breaking the Waves*) and Hassing, cross some moral line?

Prior to *Breaking the Waves*, he was no stranger to using dangerous methods to obtain intense performances. In *Epidemic*, he actually hypnotised an actress, Gitte Lind, into thinking she had contracted the plague, and she became hysterical, on camera. Even then, before Dogma, according to Stevenson, 'this conformed with von Trier's stated goal that he didn't want actors playing parts but instead wanted real people experiencing real emotions.' At Cannes, 'an energetic discussion went around film writers as to whether Gitte Lind was the world's best actress or had been genuinely hypnotised.' Shades of the 'actress' Björk, or the raw intensity of trained professionals like Watson and Jørgensen and Hassing.

Whatever one thinks of von Trier's methods, one has to admire his results. If the character of Susanne was temporarily 'demolished', Hassing still delivered an extraordinary performance, brimming with love and compassionate sensitivity. Cartlidge is more reserved, but moving nonetheless. And the three leads give what one suspects were and will be the performances of their lives. Since Björk has renounced acting, that's easy to say for her, with the Best Actress prize from Cannes in her pocket (that she wasn't even nominated for an Oscar speaks to Hollywood, not to her performance). Watson has done great work since, but nothing like this. I don't know Jørgensen's Danish career, on stage or screen, but if she has touched deeper chords of raw emotion, it would be frightening to see.

Whether the director used unduly harsh or manipulative methods to elicit those performances depends on the evidence presented in the journal and *The Humiliated* and on one's knowledge of other directors' methods. Sometimes the actors on *The Idiots*' set, especially Knud Romer Jørgensen, accused von Trier of excessive sarcasm, which he first excused – 'I am in the end nice to everyone – I try, at least' – but then dismissed: 'Screw it, I am who I am – accept it.' And sometimes he blames the actors: 'There were clashes because they were allowed to show their inner idiots, and they were so unpleasant to me.'

Bodil Jørgensen, for her part, did not feel abused. She was able to argue her own point of view about what she regarded as excesses in von Trier's script, not just from a personal standpoint but from a better understanding of what Karen the character would do in a situation. The most lurid example was that von Trier's script had Karen naked and masturbating in the orgy scene. In the film, Karen remains clothed and apart, and according to both von Trier's journal and Jørgensen's interview with Kelly, it was an amicable, mutual decision to make that change.

Jørgensen is also understanding about von Trier's failure to merge himself into the group, and the inherently voyeuristic role of the director. At the depths of his despair, Jørgensen says, 'I felt very sympathetic towards him. But, you know, as a director, he can never be part of us. But he took up the camera, and I think that helped him. Because he saw it all.'

Very occasionally his treatment of Hassing seems cruel: at one point near the end he growls to her that 'in four and half hours, it will be gone for good', probably meaning their relationship, which at that point she might have interpreted as a threat or a promise, but which was perhaps

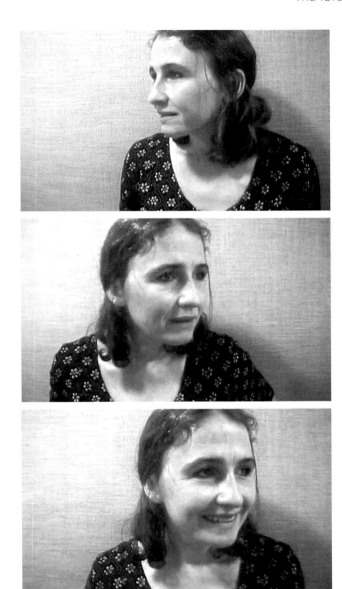

Bodil Jørgensen's virtuosity

calculated to upset her and hence elicit emotion, or more precisely tears. But by and large his methods seem compatible with how other strong directors work, although perhaps more intense and calculated and emotional and, in the end, effective.

Apart from sometimes successful, sometimes futile appeals to professionalism, von Trier's methods seemed fairly standard, no matter how intensely he applied them. The core group of actors *were* professionals, trained at the Danish National Theatre School in Copenhagen and active previously on stage or, in a few cases, screen (Hassing had made a film, *La Douleur de l'amour*, and apparently excited similar fantasies from its director, Niels Malmros).

Following the spirit and rules of Dogma involved placing considerable trust in the actors. Von Trier would set up a situation in the script – the forest scene, for instance – explain it to them and then allow them to improvise, following them with his camera. The length and low cost of the video cassettes allowed for long takes and numerous retakes, and often, to von Trier's pleasure, each new version of a scene would pare down the dialogue to a further minimum.

It was in the scenes, crucial to the film, requiring great tearful depths of emotion that the director would bring in his heavier psychological artillery, especially with Hassing. One such scene comes when, after the orgy, Jeppe and Josephine begin their spassing love scene that morphs into a true love scene, back in their 'real' characters. The sexual tension is made of shyness and hesitation; hardly a word is spoken; the tenderness of Josephine's nakedness breaks the heart. The eroticism is undeniable, yet never explicit, and the two actors, Kaas and Louise Mieritz, were apparently able to play it with a minimum of personal trauma. They handled the sequel to that scene beautifully as well – the helpless submission of Josephine to her father and Jeppe's sudden outburst from dull passivity to violent, futile grief. Afterwards, von Trier was fascinated that in a film with hardly any actual love scenes, 'it hardly takes a milligram of love in a little corner to make you burst out in tears'.

The emotional torrent of the final scene in Karen's parents' home is set up by her farewell to the group. Jørgensen delivers this with impressive control and tremulous feeling, even managing to sound utterly convincing in the sentimental line (slightly less sentimental in the script) about Susanne, who 'smiles at everyone so that the very heavens shine down on us' – shades of those heavenly bells in *Breaking the Waves*.

But the pillars of the entire film, the scenes which give it its status as a cinematic landmark and provide the crucial counterweight to the off-putting cavortings of the communal idiots, are those of naked emotional grief and compassion between Karen and Susanne. Von Trier knew that only if a viewer senses the truest, deepest complicity between those two characters, and how complicity can shade into eroticism, would the scenes, and the film, succeed. Yet he became convinced that there was tension, or at least some sort of inner holding-back, between the two actresses. 'In one way or another,' he wrote as they anticipated the first alcove scene (originally shot on the stairway), 'I've felt a kind of reserve, a strange reserve between Anne Louise and Bodil – especially on the part of Anne Louise, but also on the part of Bodil.'

That short alcove scene took days to prepare and shoot, delayed in part because of Jørgensen's small son's high fever, which no doubt figured into the intensity of her performance. To unblock Hassing, von Trier took his directorial interventions to the point of amateur therapy, as he readily admits. 'We spoke for a long time about her childhood and all sorts of things, and a little therapist was born in me.'

This is pretty problematic. It presupposes a romantic, post-1960s' and maybe naive faith in the benefits of unblocking the emotions, the injurious effects of repression and the value of a well-meaning layman monkeying with people's psyches. At one point he says, self-deprecatingly:

I don't know much about actors' methods of working. But I know that for scenes with tears, most of them use a private pain, hidden, about which they never speak, and they reach within themselves to be able to cry more or less on command … In reality it's perhaps necessary to resort to a trick, to tell a completely different story, to which they can transfer their private pain and thus enter into the situation.

Karen and Susanne

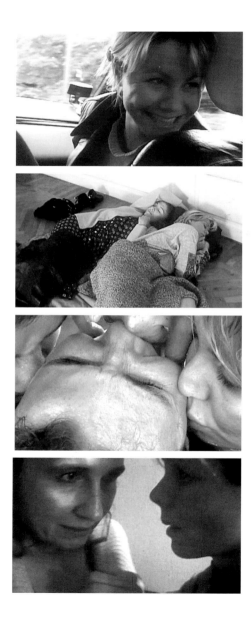

In the scene where Karen sits alone at the window and first begins to spass, Jørgensen found herself blocked until, from deep within, the memory of an old Lutheran hymn from her childhood prompted the emotions to pour forth. Von Trier refers to Josephine's tears during her love scene with Jeppe as an 'unblocking of the traumas of her childhood'.

In Hassing's case, his perhaps clumsy manipulations seem to have worked. Without warning, von Trier reports, her tears sprang forth and, 'crying madly', she went back to her youth and her disappointments. In retrospect, however, von Trier did seem to worry about his methods: 'It was very exciting,' he said of Hassing's outburst of tears. 'But in my opinion not far from sadism.' For the most part, however, if he had concerns about messing deep down inside the psyche of a young actress to achieve his desired results, he doesn't reveal them; indeed, he's convinced he did Hassing good. 'I extracted from Susanne exactly what I wanted and even though it involved two–three hours and cost at least an hour and a half of tape, it was a very pleasant and encouraging feeling to liberate certain things that apparently had nothing to do with the film.'

The trouble is, he still seems torn about what he calls his 'therapeutic genius'. On the one hand, there are his cold detachment and deliberate attempts to trick his actors into compliance. On the other, excessive complicity in these therapeutic experiments. In principle, he believes therapists must remain aloof, avoiding all their patients' pain. 'The one thing you have to know as a therapist is that you have to be completely cold when people cry,' he told me. 'They look at their watches and want people to get on with the sad stuff. A therapist needs to be cruel. I don't think I'm cruel. If you can compare it to anything, it's like a hypnotist, who can only take you where you want to go.' So maybe Lind wanted to believe she had the plague, or maybe she wasn't really hypnotised after all.

Von Trier called the final scene of *The Idiots*, in which Karen confronts her family, 'the main moment of the film'. But it was just the sort of risky scene, difficult to achieve, that von Trier has said the students at his film school were warned not to attempt – a single scene whose success or failure would define the entire movie.

Jørgensen was able to summon up her recent concerns for her own son. At Karen's parents' house, von Trier slipped in the photo of a baby and filmed an unscripted scene, which Jørgensen had not expected, of Karen looking at the photo. For Jørgensen then, the tears came easy – not to denigrate her professionalism or the intensity of her performance – and this was followed immediately by the scene of consolation with Hassing and Jørgensen, Jørgensen's face bathed in tears and Hassing looking on, mouth open, for all the world like the floating foetus at the end of *2001*. Von Trier was bemused that Hassing found it within her private reservoirs to summon up the necessary emotion. 'She cried for half an hour and it was fantastic.' Could such uncontrolled emotion unbalance a real person? Actors are a different breed, perhaps, and therapy argues that self-liberation is good. Whether or not the kind of emotion shown by Jørgensen and Hassing was good or bad for their souls, it was good for the movie.

Karen and Susanne then proceed into the living room for Karen's, and the film's, final spass. Here the intensity is almost unbearable, von Trier's camera swinging back and forth between the cake squeezing out of Karen's mouth and Susanne on the couch, her eyes brimming with tears. Von Trier knew that Karen's spassing would be the ultimate violation of the social contract, and of the implicit barriers between screen and audience – the true emergence of an inner idiot so magical (he found himself getting involved in shamanistic experiments during the editing) that it would free her from her repressive husband and family, liberate her and validate Stoffer's theories.

But suddenly von Trier felt that Hassing was freezing up, unable to let loose the kind of bottomless emotion he required. He struggled to speak impersonally to her, 'to set in motion some sort of professional standard'. They cry and shout together, effectively 'demolishing for the rest of the week the character of Susanne'. And then Hassing falls ill, or 'apparently falls ill'. She is hospitalised for suspected appendicitis and other undefined stomach pains. If he suspected her problems were psychosomatic, he doesn't admit it. He decided that she had a good side and a bad side, and that the good side was when she let her emotions out, physically represented by her mouth being half-open, and her bad side was when she closed down, represented by a mouth firmly shut.

When Hassing returned to the set, first to film the short scene in which Henrik fails to spass in front of the ladies of his art class, she seemed so frozen emotionally that he had to reassign some of her lines to others. 'The bitch is back,' grumbled von Trier to his journal dictaphone, but 'she wasn't present.'

Returning to the final scene, there was more pyschodrama; to her annoyance, von Trier even wrote Hassing a letter containing 'some good advice about what I found she needed to do with her therapy in the future'. And then, the next day, inexplicably to von Trier, it all clicked: Hassing's 'good side' (in the director's Manichaean analysis of Hassing's character) came out and she cried and cried, 'her mouth open and everything'.

If this is to be called manipulative, it is still manipulation of complicity and sympathy, and at least for art, if not necessarily for life, it works. Von Trier, speaking to Peter Øvig Knudsen, and speaking not only of *The Idiots* and Dogma but of his own amateur therapy as well:

My films have become highly moral recently … The moral is that you can practise the technique – the Dogma technique or the idiot technique – from now to kingdom come without anything coming out of it unless you have a profound, passionate desire and need to do so. Karen discovers that she needs the technique, and therefore it changes her life.

One wonders if all the leading actresses who are attracted to work with von Trier, despite his negative and perhaps misunderstood reputation, want to change their lives too.

## Epilogue: Beyond Dogma, beyond Film

Can *The Idiots*, as a radical reduction to the essence of film, lead fruitfully to future projects on a grander scale, even projects beyond film? Von Trier has already undertaken work that has exploded out of austerity, some of it seemingly far afield from film. And the very distance of that work from *The Idiots* and what we think we know about von Trier can cast light back onto his tangible achievements thus far, his earlier films and television shows, and allow them to be seen afresh.

*Dogville* and its sequels, von Trier's Nicole Kidman vehicles, represent an escalation of forces beyond a budgetarily modest little Danish Dogma film like *The Idiots*. So did *Dancer in the Dark*. Even as Dogma was being born, von Trier was contemplating experiments that took him far beyond its strictures. In 1996 he staged an art installation called *Psychomobile No. 1: The Clock of the World*, and *Dancer in the Dark* was in the works. Along with the planned 2006 production of Wagner's *Ring*, all three projects, in three different mediums, show von Trier seeking new outlets for his teeming artistic imagination – trying to find expression for all those ideas buzzing around in his head, in Emily Watson's affectionate memory.

But as regards someone who likes to 'master' things that he understands, how to explain von Trier's restless need to expand his field of activity? To most people he is known for his feature films. But he has shot many television commercials, student films and short films, and with his Filmbyen partners he has produced everything from soap operas to pornography. His art installation, *Dancer in the Dark* and especially the *Ring* represent extensions of his creative imagination beyond the comfortable mastery that he says he needs to escape his demons.

Not only work but control might seem an effective self-therapeutic technique, but he seems determined to ease his iron grip over his feature films and to extend his reach from the film he knows to the art, musicals and opera that he does not. That is why *Breaking the Waves* represented a liberation, one that he expanded upon in *The Idiots*. 'Maybe it's good to renounce power or to share it, as I did with some of the actors of *Breaking*

Von Trier: what lies beyond
film? (© Film Four Ltd, 2001)

*the Waves*,' he told Björkman. 'It was an important discovery for me. I have distanced myself more and more from the total domination that I sought in my first films.' Or at least so he says.

Still, the entire movement away from control since the mid-1990s, from complicity with the actors in *Breaking the Waves* to the communal experiments of *The Idiots* to the insane ambition of the 100-camera musical numbers in *Dancer in the Dark*, might seem to play directly into his phobias. Unless it is work itself, not the brute domination of his collaborators, that really counts. It was Baz Luhrmann, of all people – the man of truly impossible projects, like *Moulin Rouge* and *La Bohème* on Broadway – who said sympathetically of von Trier (in a conversation with *New York Times* editors in 2002) that his entire creative method seems to be to set himself apparently unrealisable goals and then to make art of the effort to realise them. 'I do like to take on these big tasks, like climbing Mount Everest or something,' von Trier responded to me.

The first of these evolutionary experiments was *Psychomobile No. 1*, commissioned and presented by the Copenhagen Art Association in 1996. As discussed in von Trier's conversation book with Björkman and seen in Björkman's film documentary *Tranceformer* (1997), it was what might be called a peopled installation. The event took place in a house with 19 rooms and involved 53 actors who played before an audience that could follow an individual performer, stay put in a single room or whatever.

In distant New Mexico – chosen for its 'mythic' quality, said von Trier – a video camera was perched on an ant hill, transmitting images of a teeming swarm of ants. Superimposed on the screen was a grid of 19 squares, corresponding to the 19 rooms of the building. Whenever a square was crossed by seven ants, one of four lamps in the relevant room – red, green, yellow, blue – would change colour. Von Trier had designed the décor and cast the performers and made up a complicated schema whereby each character was linked to others and assigned personality traits that would correspond with the colours.

Just how 'good' it was, I cannot say from personal experience. But the installation was a big hit, and the filmic record looks lively and compelling. One favourable Danish review, quoted in Stevenson, cited the obvious metaphorical implications of the ants and made the somewhat shaky leap to a post-nuclear apocalypse: 'The ants have taken power, as they will do when people have been bombed out of this world.' New York's weekly *Village Voice* was more overtly enthusiastic: 'With his odd linkage of social insects, technology, and human behavior, von Trier constructed a compelling image of a fractalized society – and a system for controlling chaos that made perfect if slightly demented cosmic sense.'

The importance of *Psychomobile No. 1* – von Trier hoped that others would take up the idea – was that it showed even at the austere ground zero of Dogma, as epitomised by the manifesto and *The Idiots*, von Trier was already thinking of how the flexibility and directness of Dogma could be applied to spectacles far larger and more complex than a Dogma film. A point noted by the *Village Voice* as far back as 1996: 'This exhibition rearranges the mental landscape. Liberated from cinematic constraints, its physics of anxiety and psychology of miracles is even more astonishing.'

For von Trier, *Psychomobile No. 1* represented an extension beyond the familiar and more or less controllable confines of film and television. So did *Dancer in the Dark*. Von Trier has always been viscerally interested in music. Even in the pared-down situation of *The Idiots*, with its recurrent off-camera rendition of Saint-Saëns' 'The Swan', he agonised over the choice of music and where to put it. Björk's anger and von Trier's hurt reaction may contribute to his now hastening over *Dancer in the Dark* as primarily a formal experiment: 'It had the weakest story,' he says. 'The idea was to make drama work with music.' Making drama work with music is the crux of the musical, the operetta, the opera. *Dancer in the Dark* is of course far more than a mere experiment, but one can take him at his word and consider his wonderfully idiosyncratic take on the musical as an art form. Whereas before in his films music served the drama but as traditional background music, here it steps to the front in fantastically staged and choreographed sequences.

So it might have seemed a logical step for von Trier to accept Wolfgang Wagner's offer to direct Richard Wagner's *Ring*. Except that von Trier readily, almost defiantly, concedes that he has never directed any kind of work for the stage, let alone opera. The commune of idiots have been called 'holy fools', and von Trier's simple excuse for his lack of experience is to make a virtue of it. 'I hope my ignorance shall be my shield,' was the way he put it to me. He calls himself a 'pure fool', the term Wagner gives to the title character in his last opera, *Parsifal*, who, uncorrupted by the world, manages to redeem it. Siegfried in the *Ring*, for all his latter-day Nietzschean and Hitlerian connotations, is a pure fool, too, a child of nature who, because of his ignorance of fear, becomes the world's mightiest hero. Except in the end, unlike Parsifal, Siegfried fails – at least until he and the world are redeemed by Brünnhilde and by nature itself in the form of the Rhine Maidens.

The novelist and essayist James McCourt has referred, operatically, in the *Los Angeles Times Book Review*, to opera and film as the 'twin hierogamous monarchs of the coinciding arts'. Film has often been called the opera of the twentieth century. That's a little unfair to both forms: opera isn't dead, although in terms of new works that have commanded the core repertory it's been faltering since 1925, the year of the premieres of Puccini's *Turandot* and Berg's *Wozzeck*. And film has rarely been centred on music like opera. But the two forms do combine the arts in a synergistic way, and as such film represents a latter-day realisation of Wagner's *Gesamtkunstwerk*, or total work of art.

Von Trier first came to the idea of working with the composer's operas as a film director. 'I have just decided that to film Wagner, that would be the ultimate goal of my life,' he told an interviewer in the *South China Post* in 1999. 'The *Ring* cycle. I could die happy.' Never mind that this was said by a man who has claimed that he is a secret troll and that all his interviews are lies. Just how he came to Bayreuth's attention is unclear. Wolfgang Wagner, at the time of the announcement of von Trier's engagement to direct the 2006 Bayreuth *Ring*, as reported by the Associated Press, spoke of the director's 'particular affinity and artistic relation to this work'. Which, given his background and interests, does make sense.

Von Trier's connections to Germany run deep. Trier, he tells us, is a Jewish name. He grew up thinking his father was Jewish, or half-Jewish; his family fled to Sweden during World War II to escape the Nazis and to work with the Danish resistance. There is a particularly harrowing concentration camp scene in *Europa*. So von Trier was raised to be dubious about the Germans and believe he was Jewish; it was only in full adulthood that his mother told him that his biological father – who has refused to have anything to do with him (more grist for the therapist) – was Christian. That is, Aryan.

Yet in his professional life he has worked closely with Germany, so geographically near Denmark. As Stevenson put it: 'For von Trier, Germany *is* Europe in many respects.' In film school he adopted the utterly spurious 'von', partly in emulation of Sternberg and Stroheim. One of his early short films (57 minutes) from 1982 was called *Images of a Liberation*, and involved a heady mixture of courage, guilt, seductive women, a Nazi soldier and his divine redemption. Much of his work since has been co-produced by a typical Euro-cocktail of television stations and producers from many countries, including Germany. He has German friends and colleagues: the actor Udo Kier, for instance, who has appeared in many of his films (including a scary appearance as the sadistic junk-freighter captain in *Breaking the Waves*).

One German writer puckishly noted that if von Trier wasn't necessarily prepared for Wagner, he was at least prepared for Bayreuth, with its own soap opera family traumas, wherein the children and nieces of Wolfgang, born in 1919, have defiantly (and unsuccessfully) challenged his leadership for years. Jens Jessen, writing in *Die Zeit*, suggested that *The Kingdom*, with its catacombs of rooms and tunnels and elevator shafts and sub-basements, its spirits, monsters, loonies and 'Mongol' oracles, was not far from the idyllic little upper-Bavarian town of Bayreuth.

If *Golden Heart* for von Trier was 'martyrdom in its purest form', then one can make an equation between martyrdom and sacrificial redemption. Redemption occurs in all of Wagner's operas, and when men do it – Walther in *Die Meistersinger von Nürnberg*, Parsifal – they come out alive. The rest – Senta, Elizabeth, Elsa, Sieglinde, Brünnhilde, Isolde, Kundry – all die in the act of sacrificing themselves for the hero. Death is martyrdom in its purest form.

The sacrificial death of women is a mainstay of Romantic art, not just Wagner's. Giselle dies to save Albrecht. Gretchen dies at Faust's callous hands and then leads him to heaven. In Italian opera, heroines drop like flies whether or not they're redeeming errant males. Death itself seems sufficiently pitiable south of the Alps to constitute operatic tragedy; the Germans (and Danes) need a moral. Feminist critics, of opera and Wagner and Romantic art in general, have taken unkindly to this behaviour. From the French Cathérine Clément to the American Susan McClary, they have attacked such art as a psychosexually sick debasement of women. Needless to say, the politically correct have likewise looked askance at von Trier's *Golden Heart* trilogy. The emotional extremes in which von Trier's helpless heroines are placed, not to speak of the horrible deaths of Bess and Selma, are what make his films controversial. Even *The Idiots*, which can be seen as Karen's victory.

Film directors have struggled as opera directors, largely because of the extreme disparity in scale of the two mediums. Opera in the nineteenth century, with its stentorian, semaphoric acting styles and cardboard-painted flats, is a long way from the naturalism of film. But film does not have to conform to the psychologically realistic, naturalistic presuppositions behind too much Anglo-American theatre; it can be abstract or futuristic or fantastical. In his earlier genre trilogy and in the 'abstraction', as he called it, of *Dancer in the Dark*, von Trier seems perfectly comfortable transcending naturalism, and that may allow him success on the modern operatic stage.

But it is the very intense, direct humanism of Dogma and *The Idiots* that provides the closest link between Wagner and von Trier. The very naked emotion of Karen and Susanne allows for von Trier's film to be reimagined as a form of latter-day Wagnerism. Music becomes tears; tears are music.

It might seem ironic that von Trier's film with the least music is his most emotional, most operatic. That is because, through the purity of Dogma principles, the sagacity of von Trier's writing and directing, the extreme close-ups of his camerawork, and the overwhelming performances of Bodil Jørgensen and the beleaguered Anne Louise Hassing, their feminine emotion substitutes for Wagner's music in a new kind of artistic synthesis. Stoffer and his masculine intellectual conceits crumble and fall, like Wagner's gods; female emotion triumphs, as in Brünnhilde's 'redemption through love' theme at the very end of the *Ring*. Wagner's marriage of the masculine and feminine in the 'total work of art' is reinvented for a new technology in a new time.

Taking on Wagner attests to von Trier's extreme romantic risk-taking, his insatiable unwillingness to rest content with what he has accomplished. What makes him special, beyond the sheer quality of his films, the power of the performances he elicits and the fecundity of his artistic imagination, is his unpredictability. But one can be assured that his twists and turns, his triumphs and misfires, his good taste and bad, will generate an excitement achieved by few other artists, in film and beyond.

# Appendix: The Dogma 95 Manifesto and the Vow of Chastity

DOGMA 95

… is a collective of film directors founded in Copenhagen in spring 1995.

DOGMA 95 has the expressed goal of countering 'certain tendencies' in the cinema today.

DOGMA 95 is a rescue action!

In 1960 enough was enough! The movie was dead and called for resurrection. The goal was correct but the means were not! The new wave proved to be a ripple that washed ashore and turned to muck.

Slogans of individualism and freedom created works for a while, but no changes. The wave was up for grabs, like the directors themselves. The wave was never stronger than the men behind it. The anti-bourgeois cinema itself became bourgeois, because the foundations upon which its theories were based was the bourgeois perception of art. The auteur concept was bourgeois romanticism from the very start and thereby … false!

To DOGMA 95 cinema is not individual!

Today a technological storm is raging, the result of which will be the ultimate democratisation of the cinema. For the first time, anyone can make movies. But the more accessible the media becomes, the more important the avant-garde. It is no accident that the phrase 'avant-garde' has military connotations. Discipline is the answer … we must put our films into uniform, because the individual film will be decadent by definition!

DOGMA 95 counters the individual film by the principle of presenting an indisputable set of rules known as THE VOW OF CHASTITY.

In 1960 enough was enough! The movie had been cosmeticised to death, they said; yet since then the use of cosmetics has exploded.

The 'supreme' task of the decadent film-makers is to fool the audience. Is that what we are so proud of? Is that what the '100 years' have brought us? Illusions via which emotions can be communicated? … By the individual artist's free choice of trickery?

Predictability (dramaturgy) has become the golden calf around which we dance. Having the characters' inner lives justify the plot is too complicated, and not 'high art'. As never before, the superficial action and the superficial movie are receiving all the praise.

The result is barren. An illusion of pathos and an illusion of love.

To DOGMA 95 the movie is not illusion!

Today a technological storm is raging of which the result is the elevation of cosmetics to God. By using new technology anyone at any time can wash the last grains of truth away in the deadly embrace of sensation. The illusions are everything the movie can hide behind.

DOGMA 95 counters the film of illusion by the presentation of an indisputable set of rules known as THE VOW OF CHASTITY.

**The Vow of Chastity**

'I swear to submit to the following set of rules drawn up and confirmed by DOGMA 95:

1. Shooting must be done on location. Props and sets must not be brought in (if a particular prop is necessary for the story, a location must be chosen where this prop is to be found).

2. The sound must never be produced apart from the images or vice versa. (Music must not be used unless it occurs where the scene is being shot.)

3. The camera must be hand-held. Any movement or immobility attainable in the hand is permitted. (The film must not take place where the camera is standing; shooting must take place where the film takes place.)

4. The film must be in color. Special lighting is not acceptable. (If there is too little light for exposure the scene must be cut or a single lamp be attached to the camera.)

5. Optical work and filters are forbidden.

6. The film must not contain superficial action. (Murders, weapons, etc. must not occur.)

7. Temporal and geographical alienation are forbidden. (That is to say that the film takes place here and now.)

8. Genre movies are not acceptable.

9. The film format must be Academy 35 mm.

10. The director must not be credited.

Furthermore I swear as a director to refrain from personal taste! I am no longer an artist. I swear to refrain from creating a 'work', as I regard the instant as more important than the whole. My supreme goal is to force the truth out of my characters and settings. I swear to do so by all the means available and at the cost of any good taste and any aesthetic considerations.

Thus I make my VOW OF CHASTITY.'

Copenhagen, Monday 13 March 1995
On behalf of DOGMA 95

Lars von Trier  Thomas Vinterberg

# Credits

**Idioterne/Dogma 2:**
**The Idiots**

Denmark/France/Italy/
Netherlands/Germany/
Sweden
1998

**Director**
Lars von Trier
**Producer**
Vibeke Windeløv
**Screenplay**
Lars von Trier
**Director of Photography**
Lars von Trier
**Editor**
Molly Malene Stensgaard

©Zentropa Entertainments2
ApS and La Sept Cinéma
**Production Companies**
Produced by Zentropa
Entertainments2 ApS and
DR TV in co-production with
Liberator Productions,
S.a.r.l., La Sept Cinéma,
Argus Film Produktie, VPRO
Television, Holland,
ZDF/ARTE with the support
of Nordic Film and
Television Fund, CoBO
Fund, Holland in
collaboration with SVT
Drama, Canal+ (France),
RAI Cinema Fiction, 3
Emme Cinematografica
**Executive Producers**
Peter Aalbæk Jensen
DR TV:

Svend Abrahamsen
Nordic Film & TV Fund:
Dag Alveberg
**Assistants to Producer**
Paris:
Nynne Oldenburg
Mette Nelund
**Co-producers**
Marianne Slot
Peter van Vogelpoel
Erik Schut
**Accountants**
Ann Køj Slemming
Ann Vognsen
**Production Manager**
Lene Nielsen
**Post-production**
**Co-ordinator**
Lene Irgens
**Production Assistant**
Tine Grew Pfeiffer
**Assistant Directors**
Kristoffer Nyholm
Jesper Jargil
Casper Holm
**Casting**
Rie Hedegaard
**Script/Editing Consultant**
Mogens Rukov
**Camera Operators**
Kristoffer Nyholm
Jesper Jargil
Casper Holm
**Camera Assistants**
Edvard Friss-Møller
Ian Hansen
**Clapper/Materials**
**Recorder**
Caroline Cogez
**Stills Photographer**
Jan Schut

**Assistant Editors**
Anne Hovad Fisher
Carsten Søsted
**Melodica Player**
Kim Kristensen
**Soundtrack**
'The Swan' by Camille Saint-
Saëns; 'Vi er dem de andre
ikke må lege med' by Kim
Larsen, Erik Clausen
**Sound Designer**
Per Streit
**Sound Engineers**
Kristian Eidnes Andersen
Johan Winbladh
**Boom Operators**
John Nielsen
Rene Schrøder
**English Translation**
Jonathan Sydenham
**Catering**
'Petite' Buch Petersen
**Avid Consultant**
Pelle Folmer
**Online Facilities**
Feltwawe A/S
**Video Transfer to 35 mm**
**Film**
Hokus Bogus ApS
**Laboratory**
Johan Ankerstjerne A/S
**Sound Studio**
Mainstream ApS
**Post-production Planning**
**System**
London B&B Systems Ltd
**Public Relations**
Christel Hammer
**Legal Adviser**
Lene Børglum

**The Idiots Wish to Thank**
Niels Vørsel
Bent Hassing
Søllerød Kro
Jægersborg Skov Distrikt
Rockwool
**International Sales**
Trust Film Sales ApS

**Cast**
**Bodil Jørgensen**
Karen
**Jens Albinus**
Stoffer
**Anne Louise Hassing**
Susanne
**Troels Lyby**
Henrik
**Nikolaj Lie Kaas**
Jeppe
**Louise Mieritz**
Josephine
**Henrik Prip**
Ped
**Luis Mesonero**
Miguel
**Knud Romer Jørgensen**
Axel
**Trine Michelsen**
Nana
**Anne-Grethe Bjarup Riis**
Katrine
**Paprika Steen**
Vibeke, prospective house
buyer
**Erik Wedersøe**
Svend, Stoffer's uncle
**Michael Moritzen**
man from Søllerød
municipality

**Anders Hove**
Josephine's father
**Jan Elle**
waiter
**Claus Strandberg**
guide at factory
**Jens Jørgen Spottag**
boss at advertising agency
**John Martinus**
man in morning-jacket
**Lars Bjarke**
rocker 1
**Ewald Larsen**
rocker 2
**Christian Friis**
rocker 3
**Louise B. Clausen**
Linda, rocker girl
**Hans Henrik Clemensen**
Anders, Karen's husband
**Lone Lindorff**
Karen's mother
**Erno Müller**
Karen's grandfather
**Regitze Estrup**
Louise, Karen's sister
**Lotte Munk**
Britta, Karen's sister
**Marina Bouras**
Axel's wife
**Julie Wieth**
woman with two kids
**Kirsten Vaupel**
art class lady 1
**Lillian Tillegren**
art class lady 2
**Birgit Conradi**
art class lady 3
**Peter Frøge**
man in swimming pool

**Albert Wickmann**
prospective house buyer
**Ditlev Weddelsborg**
Severin at advertising
agency
**Jesper Sønderaas**
Svendsen at advertising
agency
**Svend Erik Plannthin**
**Torben Meyrowitsch**
**Lis Bente Petersen**
**Palle Lorentz Emiliussen**
**Axel Schmidt**
Mongols
**Iris Albøge**
qualified carer

*[uncredited]*
**Bent Sørensen**
taxi driver
**Lars von Trier**
voice of interviewer

**10,280 feet**
**114 minutes 13 seconds**
**Dolby**
**In Colour**
**Subtitles**

In line with the collaborative
ideals of Dogma 95 the cast
and crew are credited
together under the heading
'made by'. Lars von Trier
himself is not credited at all.

Credits compiled by
Markku Salmi,
BFI Filmographic Unit

# Bibliography and Sources

Björkman, Stig, *Tranceformer* (1997). Film documentary about von Trier.

——, *Trier om von Trier, Samtal med Stig Björkman* (Stockholm: Alfabeta, 1999). Translated as *Entretiens avec Lars von Trier* (Paris: Cahiers du Cinéma, 2000).

Durbin, Karen, 'Making the Waves', *New York Times Magazine*, 30 April 2000.

——, 'Second Sight', Playbill programme book for the New York Film Festival, September 2000.

Jargil, Jesper, *The Humiliated* (1998), *The Exhibited* (2000) and *The Purified* (2002). Film documentaries about *The Idiots*, *Psychomobile No. 1* and the Dogma 'brotherhood' respectively.

Jensen, Hans, *Barnet og Idioten: Danske Dogmefilm i Naerbilleder* (Arhus: Systime, 2001).

Kelly, Richard, *The Name of This Book Is Dogme 95* (London: Faber and Faber, 2000).

Nelson, Victoria, *The Secret Life of Puppets* (Cambridge, MA: Harvard University Press, 2001).

Rockwell, John, 'Von Trier and Wagner, a Bond Sealed in Emotion', *New York Times Arts & Leisure* section, 8 April 2001.

——, 'Lars von Trier, Bayreuth and the "*Ring*"', *Opera* magazine (London), January 2002.

——, Interview with Lars von Trier, Copenhagen, 26 March 2002, notes.

Schepelern, Peter, *Lars von Triers Film: Tvang og Befrielse* (Copenhagen: Rosinante, 2000).

Stevenson, Jack, *Lars von Trier* (London: BFI World Directors, 2002).

Von Trier, Lars, *Idioterne: Manuskript, Dagbog* (Copenhagen: Sammlerens Bogklub, 1998). Translated as *Les Idiots: Journal intime & Scénario* (Paris: Atelier Alpha Bleue, 1998).

www.dogme95.dk – Official Dogma 95 website, including articles and interviews with von Trier.

# Also Published

**L'Argent**
Kent Jones (1999)

**Blade Runner**
Scott Bukatman (1997)

**Blue Velvet**
Michael Atkinson (1997)

**Caravaggio**
Leo Bersani & Ulysse Dutoit (1999)

**A City of Sadness**
Bérénice Reynaud (2002)

**Crash**
Iain Sinclair (1999)

**The Crying Game**
Jane Giles (1997)

**Dead Man**
Jonathan Rosenbaum (2000)

**Dilwale Dulhaniya Le Jayenge**
Anupama Chopra (2002)

**Don't Look Now**
Mark Sanderson (1996)

**Do the Right Thing**
Ed Guerrero (2001)

**Easy Rider**
Lee Hill (1996)

**The Exorcist**
Mark Kermode (1997, 2nd edn 1998)

**Eyes Wide Shut**
Michel Chion (2002)

**Heat**
Nick James (2002)

**Independence Day**
Michael Rogin (1998)

**Jaws**
Antonia Quirke (2002)

**Last Tango in Paris**
David Thompson (1998)

**Once Upon a Time in America**
Adrian Martin (1998)

**Pulp Fiction**
Dana Polan (2000)

**The Right Stuff**
Tom Charity (1997)

**Saló or The 120 Days of Sodom**
Gary Indiana (2000)

**Seven**
Richard Dyer (1999)

**The Silence of the Lambs**
Yvonne Tasker (2002)

**The Terminator**
Sean French (1996)

**Thelma & Louise**
Marita Sturken (2000)

**The Thing**
Anne Billson (1997)

**The 'Three Colours' Trilogy**
Geoff Andrew (1998)

**Titanic**
David M. Lubin (1999)

**Trainspotting**
Murray Smith (2002)

**The Usual Suspects**
Ernest Larsen (2002)

**The Wings of the Dove**
Robin Wood (1999)

**Women on the Verge of a Nervous Breakdown**
Peter William Evans (1996)

**WR – Mysteries of the Organism**
Raymond Durgnat (1999)